The Female Face
in Patriarchy

The Female Face in Patriarchy

Oppression as Culture

Frances B. O'Connor
Becky S. Drury

Michigan State University
East Lansing

∞ The paper used in this publication meets the minimum requirements of
ANSI/NISO Z39.48-1992 (R 1997) (Permanence of Paper).

03 02 01 00 99 98   1 2 3 4 5 6

Library of Congress Cataloging-in-Publication Data

O'Connor, Frances B. (Frances Bernard)
    The female face in patriarchy: oppression as culture / Frances B. O'Connor, Becky
S. Drury.
        p.   cm.
    Includes bibliographical references and index.
    ISBN 0-87013-494—(alk. Paper)
    1. Women in the Catholic Church—United States.   2. Women in the Catholic
Church—Brazil. 3. Catholic women—United States—Interviews. 4. Catholic
women—Brazil—Interviews. 5. Feminist theology. I. Drury, Becky S.
BX1407.W65036   1998
282'082—dc21   98-41217
                                                                    CIP

This book is dedicated to

Elizabeth Cady Stanton (1815–1902), who believed

that the church was the greatest barrier

to women's emancipation;

and to all those women mentors

who are committed to freeing their sisters

from the grip of male and female

patriarchal behavior in the church.

CONTENTS

ACKNOWLEDGMENTS

This book would never have come into existence were it not for:

— the women in Brazil and the United States who generously gave of themselves by participating in our interviews and sharing their experiences as both victims and perpetrators in the patriarchal system.

— the Holy Cross Sisters in Brazil and the United States who gathered the women together for interviews and who gave of their time, energy, and skills to enable us to complete our research.

— the readers, Regina A. Coll, CSJ, director of field education, Department of Theology, University of Notre Dame, Indiana; Mary Aquin O'Neill, RSM, director, Mount Saint Agnes Theological Center for Women, Baltimore, Maryland; Carol Schaal, managing editor, *Notre Dame Magazine,* University of Notre Dame, Indiana; and David Schlaver, CSC, former publisher, Ave Maria Press, Notre Dame, Indiana, who painstakingly edited our work.

— the feminist theologians, Scripture scholars, and other leading feminists in both the United States and Brazil whose insights and theories provided the framework that was enhanced by the experiences of grassroots women.

— the Kellogg Institute for International Studies at the University of Notre Dame for providing us the space and support for our work.

— the Michigan State University Press staff, i.e., Julie L. Loehr, Associate Director/Editor in Chief, Martha A. Bates, Acquisitions Editor, Annete K. Tanner, Editorial Assistant, Sandy Judd, copyeditor, and Michael Smith for their encouragement and their collaborative efforts to bring this message to publication.

— the many others, both men and women who have encouraged us in this work and cheered us on.

LEADING CONTRIBUTORS

UNITED STATES

Anne E. Carr, BVM, author, lecturer, and professor of theology at the Divinity School of the University of Chicago.

Joan Chittister, OSB, noted national and international lecturer, widely published author, executive director of Benetvision: A Resource and Research Center for Contemporary Spirituality, Erie, Penn.

Regina A. Coll, CSJ, author, lecturer, and director of field education, Department of Theology at the University of Notre Dame.

Mary Collins, OSB, author, editor, lecturer and professor of liturgical studies in the Department of Religion and Religious Education at the Catholic University of America.

Doris Donnelly, professor of theology at John Carroll University, is director of the Cardinal Suenens Program in Theology and Church Life.

Dorothy (Dody) H. Donnelly, Bernard Osher Chair of Philosophy, Fromm Institute, San Francisco. She is also professor of spirituality at Sophia Center, Holy Names College.

Ruth McDonough Fitzpatrick, former national coordinator, Women's Ordination Conference, Washington, D.C.

Elizabeth A. Johnson, CSJ, author, lecturer, and distinguished professor of theology, Fordham University.

Theresa Kane, RSM, activist and lecturer on Catholic feminism, former president of the Leadership Conference of Women Religious, Dobbs Ferry, N.Y.

Eileen McKeown, CSJ, professor of theology, Immaculate Conception Seminary, Huntington, N.Y.

Susan Muto, author, lecturer, executive director, and cofoundress of Epiphany Association, Pittsburgh, Penn.

Rosemary Radford Ruether, Georgia Harkness Professor of theology at Garrett-Evangelical Seminary, Evanston, Ill. An expert in church history and historical theology and an internationally recognized writer and lecturer on feminism and religion.

Joyce Rupp, OSM, lecturer and author of several books and journal articles as well as several cassette programs.

Sandra M. Schneiders, IHM, author, lecturer, and professor of New Testament and spirituality at the Jesuit School of Theology and Graduate Theological Union, Berkeley, Calif.

Mary Luke Tobin, SL, auditor at Vatican II and former president of the Leadership Conference of Women Religious.

Miriam Therese Winter, MMS, professor of liturgy, worship, spirituality, and feminist studies at Hartford Seminary. Author of several award-winning books.

BRAZIL

Cleide Rita Silverio de Almeida, professor in the Department of Theology and Sciences of Religion at the Catholic Pontifical University (PUC) of São Paulo. Director of the College of Administration and Accounting Sciences of Saint Francis University in São Paulo.

Marie Amelia, Cannoness of St. Augustine, psychologist and professor of religious studies.

Ana Flora Anderson, an American theologian who first went to Brazil as a Fulbright Scholar in 1960. For many years she was the only woman theologian in Brazil. Currently a theologian and New Testament Scripture scholar at Catholic University, São Paulo.

Maristela Guimaraes Andre, professor of theology and religious sciences at Catholic Pontifical University, and principal of the middle school of Colegio Santa Maria.

Nancy Pereira Cardoso, ordained presbitera in the Methodist Church of Rio de Janeiro. Presently working on her doctorate in Old Testament studies, and teacher of theology and Old Testament studies at the Methodist Institute of

Higher Education and the Theological Institute of São Paulo. She has published widely.

Tereza Maria Cavalcanti, professor and coordinator of the Graduate Department of Theology at the Catholic Pontifical University. She is also the coordinator of the Spirituality Program at CEBI—the Center for Biblical Studies. Tereza has long worked in Bible ministry among the CEBs.

CEBs, Comunidades Ecclesiales de base, Christian base communities, or, more generally, small Christian communities. CEBs are inequivocally identified as a new way of being church, as initial cells of ecclesiastical structuring and foci of evangelization and human promotion. They are community in their interpersonal relationships, ecclesial in the faith, celebration of the Word of God and unity with the mission of the Church and base as small groups forming cells in the large community.[1]

Maria Luiza Guedes Costa, professor of theology and science of religion at the Catholic Pontifical University. Consultant to the academic vice president of the university.

Maria Cecilia Domezi, former sister, theologian at the Catholic University of São Paulo. Her book *Do Corpo Cintilante ao Corpo Torturado* (*From a Scintillating Body to a Tortured Body*) was just published by Vozes.

Ivone Gebara, an Augustinian sister and one of the most esteemed women theologians in Latin America. Her areas of expertise include theology, philosophy, and anthropology. She taught theology, philosophy, and anthropology at the Theology Institute of Recife (ITER) until 1989, when the Vatican ordered ITER closed. Since then, Ivone has taught in an "underground educational circle." She lives and works in the destitute northeast. She was silenced for two years by the Vatican, beginning in September 1995.

Sister Gertrudis, sister of St. Joseph of Chambery, theologian.

Haidi Jarschel, ordained Lutheran pastora, presently teaching feminist spirituality and Old Testament studies at the Theological Institute of São Paulo. She is on the coordinating committee of *Mandragora*, a magazine founded by the Nucleus of Women's Theological Studies in Latin America (NET-MAL).

Sister Marian, provincial of the Sisters of Divine Providence, Scripture scholar.

Frances O'Gorman, a Brazilian educator who since 1976 has participated in the activities of the Ecumenical Center for Action and Reflection (CEAR)—a small, multidisciplinary group under the Federation of Organizations for Social and Educational Assistance. CEAR accompanies community groups in the hillside slums of Rio de Janeiro. Frances has lectured, conducted workshops, and acted as resource person at universities and nongovernmental agencies in several countries. She is the author of six books—two in Portuguese, two in English, and two in both languages.

Marguerite Olivia, professor of religious studies at the Catholic University of São Paulo.

Nilda Nair Reinehr, Franciscan sister, has done postgraduate work in theology and is secretary of the Missiology Department at the Assuncao College of Theology in São Paulo.

Eliad Dias Dos Santos, ordained Methodist presbitera, is presently working on her master's degree in pastoral theology. She is assistant pastora in the Methodist Church of Jabaquara, São Paulo. She contributes articles to the *Mandragora* magazine of Women's Theological Studies in Latin America and has edited a series of seven small books called "Contando Nossa Estoria" (Telling our Stories), each dealing with a problematic issue of gender.

Sonia, a Pastorinas sister, teaches Scripture at the Dominican School of Theology.

NOTE

1. Taken from Robert S. Pelton, CSC, *From Power to Communion: Toward a New Way of Being Church Based on the Latin American Experience* (South Bend, Ind.: University of Notre Dame Press, 1994), xv. Also, Frances O'Gorman, *Base Communities in Brazil,* (Ventnor, New Jersey: Overseas Ministries Study Center, December 1983), 30.

INTRODUCTION

Patriarchal oppression in the Catholic church is ordinarily attributed to men, and to clerics in particular. However, during interviews for a previous book (*Like Bread Their Voices Rise, Global Women Challenge the Church*, Ave Maria Press, 1993), women on four continents frequently identified the patriarchal behavior of other women as a major obstacle to women's equality.

These conversations raised our awareness to the fact that the problem of patriarchy is more complicated than we had originally thought. As we became aware of the complexity of women's participation and role in fostering their own oppression, we realized that the story of women's conscious and unconscious complicity in patriarchal dominance must be told.

This book is the result of a two-year study of how and why women in the Western Hemisphere, as characterized by women in Brazil and the United States, participate in their own oppression in the Catholic Church. The purpose is to show how centuries of conditioning by the patriarchal church has made women both victims and perpetrators of oppression and that their cooperation with and submission to patriarchal dominance has been both conscious and unconscious. The book's blessing will be a new awareness among women that will enable them to cooperate and support one another in their struggle for an egalitarian church.

My colleague, Becky Drury, Ph.D., and I come to this study with differing backgrounds, experiences, and viewpoints on a number of issues relative to women's oppression of women, not the least of which is the relationship of sisters and other women. The fact that we are not only still speaking after three years, but are in fact "good friends," is proof that sisters and other women can, in Susan Muto's words, "agree to disagree agreeably." We spent endless hours sharing our sometimes contradictory interpretations of what we heard in the

1

interviews. Our approach was to dialogue until we could hear one another's point of view. This process deeply enriched our analysis and conclusions, providing us with new insights regarding our own participation in patriarchal oppression. It also deepened our understanding of what friendship and collaboration between sisters and other women can mean. Because of our different gifts, I drafted each chapter while Becky was the chief editor. The resulting chapters frequently bore little resemblance to the original drafts.

Data was gathered through personal interviews. The sampling was selective but typical of women in parish settings and small communities in both countries. We interviewed leading Catholic feminists in each country regarding their theories as to why women are co-opted into the patriarchal system. No one claimed to have done extensive research on the question, but each gave her insights and told of her experiences. We then interviewed over two hundred women in each country with the purpose of challenging and/or corroborating the assumptions of the leading feminists by the experiences of grassroots sisters and other women.

The interviews provided a vehicle for women to gather and tell their stories. In the process many began to realize what was happening to them and, more importantly, what they were doing to other women. For some, it was very difficult to admit their own oppressive behavior; a few denied that they had ever been oppressed, nor did they acknowledge they had ever oppressed another woman. The examples cited in the following chapters provide a variety of perspectives and insights regarding women's use and misuse of power. Because so many women found the courage to articulate and reflect on their experiences, it was possible for us to gain some common understandings regarding their motives.

The book is divided into three parts: (1) How women in the United States see their participation in patriarchal oppression; (2) Brazilian women's insights into their cooperation in the double bind of machismo and patriarchy; (3) A profile of patriarchal women, indicating the similarities and differences evidenced among women in the two countries.

There is much in these pages that you, the reader, may already know, but perhaps seeing through the eyes of these women and hearing them speak of their pain, you will be inspired to reflect on your own relationships with other women with new awareness. This alone would make all of our work worthwhile.

Frances B. O'Connor, CSC
Becky S. Drury, Ph.D.
Kellogg Institute
University of Notre Dame
January 1998

PART I

THE FACES OF UNITED STATES WOMEN

So perverted is the religious element in women's nature that with faith and works she is the chief support of the church and clergy; the very powers that make her emancipation impossible.

Elizabeth Cady Stanton
The Woman's Bible

CHAPTER 1

THE AIR WE BREATHE

**Women will have the place in the church they want when they can silence
the voice that says, "You are not worthy."[1]**

Why is it that so many women across this country feel undeserving of a
more participatory role in the church? Why do some women indicate
repeatedly that their place is in the pews, that they are not holy enough to be
eucharistic ministers or intelligent enough to be in decision-making roles in
the church? More importantly, Susan Muto asks, "What has deformed women's
thinking and self-image to such an extent that they do not consider themselves
worthy?"[2]

One of the many reasons for this feeling of unworthiness is the way women
have been, and are still, treated by some of the clergy. Two experiences illustrate this assumption: First, a woman in a midwestern parish, a minister of
liturgical art responsible for decorating the church for the various feasts and
seasons of the church year, was talking to her pastor. The question of women's
role in the church surfaced in their conversation and she remarked that she did
not feel called to ordination nor was she interested in being a priest. "All I want
is a little respect," she told him. He retorted, "Why do you think you deserve
respect? You're only a woman!" Although few priests are as blatant in their
response, many women have indicated that they receive the message of their
"unworthiness" in various ways from the clergy. In a second example, a woman
eucharistic minister on the East Coast made it a practice to call each person by
name when distributing communion. The pastor disapproved and told her not
to do it because more parishioners were approaching her than him. However,
since the woman knew the people in her parish so well, she felt called to continue the practice. One Sunday she happened to be at the same communion
station as the pastor, and he heard her addressing each person by name. After
they had returned to the altar, he struck her on the arm and told her he wanted

to see her in the sacristy after Mass. The whole congregation was witness to her humiliation.

These and similar experiences are among the reasons why some women have internalized only the first part of the prayer before communion—"Lord I am not worthy"—and cannot quite believe that God has "said the word" and healed women as well as men in our church.

As this book progresses, the reader will discover why some women in Brazil and the United States, who have been victims of patriarchy for centuries, endeavor to sustain gender inequality within the patriarchal structure of the Catholic Church. Our purpose is to raise women's awareness to how they have been conditioned by the patriarchal church throughout history; to how that conditioning has caused them to be seduced into the very system that oppresses them; and to the fact that they must take responsibility for their own actions. It is not our intent to blame women for the success of the patriarchal system.

The patriarchal socialization of women has conditioned them to think, act, behave, and react as second-class members of the church. "Women are socialized to believe that they are good by accepting the dominant male view of how women ought to act," says Rosemary Radford Ruether.[3] Women have internalized the message that behavior accepted by society, the institutional church, and its leaders is what constitutes a "good woman" or a "good sister" and that any other conduct is displeasing to God. "If the normative powers of any culture tell the out-group that they are not able to do what the normative group does, then of course they believe it," states Joan Chittister.[4] This is one reason why a woman will say, "Oh, I do not think I could be a priest."

For women to exist in this suffocating atmosphere in the patriarchal church is analogous to struggling to survive in a house where carbon monoxide is spreading through every room. Patriarchy, like carbon monoxide, is insidious because it is colorless, odorless, and invisible. The human body does not detect the presence of carbon monoxide: it interprets the gas as oxygen. Likewise, women are not even aware they are absorbing patriarchy into their systems. As with the air they breathe, they take the patriarchal system for granted, rarely think of it at all—yet its effects are deadly.

Like carbon monoxide poisoning, patriarchal conditioning can be either intentional or accidental. Despite efforts in recent years by theologians and writers to raise women's awareness of the damaging effects of patriarchy, far too many women still choose to model the "good woman" in today's church. Others are unconsciously drawn to patriarchy because their conditioning is so complete. Many women have come to believe they are second-class citizens and have lost sight of the Christian teaching that we are all one in Christ Jesus.

The longer women delay addressing the lethal effects of patriarchal dominance, the greater the damage to them will be. Women's self-images become warped, bent, twisted, and paralyzed by continued exposure to this debilitating message.

Women have been conditioned by the Catholic Church to:

— relate to a male God only;
— trust in an external, superior male authority;
— believe that only males have been called by God to preside at the altar;
— believe that decision making in the church should be done by men only;
— believe that responsibility and power belong rightly to men;
— believe that the male is the norm and thus that the term "men" includes women also.

Concurrently, these same women have absorbed the message that:

— women's place is only in the home;
— volunteer service in the church is a privilege;
— the more humble women are, the holier they are;
— women's role is to be secondary and supportive;
— a silent, passive, and obedient Mary is the model for "good women";
— "good women" do not question the priest's, the bishop's, or the pope's pronouncements.

These presumptions reinforce patterns of dependency and passivity that keep women in a state of mental "unworthiness." For many women the church is their security; they know their place and accept the structure. Some women embrace the hierarchical system, wanting and needing someone to define appropriate behavior and hold them accountable. In doing so, they sustain the very institution that keeps them oppressed. The passivity that results from patriarchal conditioning often produces behavior like that of a woman in Baltimore who told a friend who was questioning the actions of the clergy to calm down, center herself, and she'd see that everything in the church was okay. "It's you who have the problems," she said.

This patriarchal conditioning has so debilitated some women that they continually look to the clergy for approval. Joan Chittister, OSB, observes that there are women all over this country who are afraid to admit they are feminists or that they desire equal participation in their church. They are afraid, not just because their husbands or women friends would be furious, but also because their pastor might say, "Oh, don't tell me you are one of *those*!" Consequently, these women internalize the message that they are inferior. They bow down to stunted expectations and look to the clergy for approval.[5] They keep quiet and do what a "good woman" or a "good sister" in the church is expected to do. They do not rock the boat, and they continue to inhale the debilitating air of patriarchy.

As with carbon monoxide poisoning, the effects of patriarchal dominance can sometimes be reversed. Both maladies respond to deep draughts of oxygen. Thirty years ago, Pope John XXIII tried to open the windows of the church to let in fresh air. Yet today women are still being asphyxiated. The windows remain closed, locked, and sealed against the message of Jesus for women. Continued clerical dominance is depriving women of the very breath of life and depriving the universal church of the richness of their gifts. The clerical voice that inundates women with the poison of "you are not worthy" will only be silenced when women unite, break open the sealed windows, and inhale the fresh air of equality. Only then will they be able to assume their rightful place in the church.

Is there no other way to describe patriarchy than as a deadly fume that cripples women's minds and intellects or as a poison that has deformed women's images of themselves and their God? Both male and female theologians have offered valuable insights into the nature of the patriarchal dominance that has for centuries permeated the Catholic Church. Bishop P. Francis Murphy of Baltimore, an advocate for women, best described its pervasiveness when he said:

> Patriarchal dominance pervades our church, a dominance that excludes the presence, insights, and experience of women from the "table" where the formulation of the church's doctrine takes place and the exercise of its power is discerned. It likewise excludes women from presiding at the table where the community of faith is fed. This patriarchy continues to permeate the church and supports a climate that not only robs women of their full personhood, but also encourages men to be domineering, aggressive and selfish.[6]

Women were granted equality at the time of creation: "In God's image God created them; male and female God created them" [Gen 1:27]. This truth was reiterated by Paul, who stated, "There does not exist among you . . . male or female. All are one in Christ Jesus" [Gal 3:28]. Patriarchy takes away this equality. It robs women of their full personhood and relegates them to second-class membership in the church.

Rosemary Radford Ruether maintains that the nature of patriarchy is divisiveness.

> I think there are all kinds of divisiveness, and patriarchy by its very nature constructs divisiveness between all of the subgroups. That's how it conquers. It's called "divide and conquer."[7]

8

One of the most prominent examples of divisiveness the church has been successful in maintaining is that between sisters in religious orders and other women. Fear, mistrust, jealousy, and misunderstanding have characterized the relationship between these two groups of women for centuries. Chapter 5 addresses this in detail and speaks of the efforts being made to heal the rift that has separated these women in the church.

What crystallizes the heart of patriarchy for theologian Elizabeth Schüssler Fiorenza is dependence on and control by men in power. Obedience is the essence of patriarchy, she maintains. Her personal story illustrates her conviction.

> In 1963 when I completed my Master of Divinity and licentiate examinations, the Second Vatican Council received a petition to consider women's ordination to the priesthood. Since I was the first woman to receive a theological degree in Wurzburg, the faculty assured me that they would recommend me for ordination if the council approved of it. I replied that I did not think I had a vocation to become a pastor in an isolated village in the woods. However, I asserted, I do have a vocation to become a bishop. "That will never happen," the dean assured me. When I asked, "Why not?" he explained: "Because then we would depend on you and owe obedience to you."[8]

The following definition touches the heart and soul of women whose awareness has been raised: "I find patriarchy everywhere: men and the things men do have been valued a lot in every place and time, and women and the things women do have been valued less. That tilt is the essence of patriarchy."[9] Why, after almost two thousand years of Christian living, have women not been able to free themselves from the downside of that tilt? More importantly, why have some women allowed themselves to be co-opted into it?

According to Ruth McDonough Fitzpatrick, former national coordinator of the Women's Ordination Conference, co-optation is the worst problem women face in the church today. The clergy know very well how to co-opt women. They know they cannot bring in a dictator for a pastor and expect women to go along with him. So, consciously or not, they bring in someone who has a similar mind-set, who smiles and puts his arm around the women, visits them when they are sick, makes them believe they are privileged to do volunteer work. Fitzpatrick contends women accept these crumbs gladly because they have nothing else. They feel ashamed to ask to participate more or to criticize because they believe "father has been so nice to them."[10]

Gerda Lerner, in *The Creation of Patriarchy*, points out,

> The system of patriarchy, can function only with the co-operation of women. This co-operation is secured by a variety of means: gender indoctrination; educational deprivation; the denial to women of knowledge of their history; the dividing of women, one from the other, by defining "respectability" and "deviance" according to women's sexual activities; by restraints and outright coercion; by discrimination in access to economic resources and political power; and by awarding class privileges to conforming women.[11]

Women who, for example, silently submit to a domineering, authoritative, rude pastor who labels another woman a "liberal terrorist" because she speaks up at a staff meeting for inclusive language in the liturgy are cooperating with and affirming patriarchal domination. In fact, they are joining the priest publicly in his subordination of women. Many such women will later attempt to salve their consciences by telling the offended woman that they really support her views. This will allow them to maintain their image as "good women" in front of the priest. Such behavior is the ultimate in women's betrayal of women.

Those who actively join the clergy in their domination of women are exemplified by the sister who worked her way up in the diocesan structure until she was literally in charge of everything and was strategically positioned to help other women. But when the bishop wanted his secretary fired and did not want to do it himself, the sister stepped in and assigned so much work to the secretary that she finally resigned. This clerical injustice was clearly accomplished with the cooperation of a woman.

During our interviews, women in a variety of vocations across this country illustrated their internalization of the patriarchal message of "unworthiness":

> I don't think I could be a eucharistic minister. I don't feel I'm holy enough. I don't toe the line and measure up. I don't have a right to do something like that. [Young Married Woman]

> We accept a male presider who does a terrible job but refuse to consider a female presider who would do much better. [Sister]

> When I enrolled as a new member in my parish, I was told by the pastor that I could be on the decoration and altar committees. My reply was, 'That's all right because what else could I do?'[Married Woman]

Despite the avowals of church leaders about women's equality, the symbolism of a male divinity and male superiority "is so deeply embedded in Christian theology, church structure, and liturgical practice that the Christian imagination unconsciously absorbs its destructive and exclusionary messages from childhood on."[12]

Examples from the women interviewed exemplify this. A mother in Maryland told her little girl that no matter how hard she tried she would never be good because only God was good. A married woman in Pennsylvania protested that she could never be a Eucharistic minister. She didn't feel she was holy enough because she hadn't dedicated her life to God like the priests had. "I don't feel I have a right to do something like that," she said. Consider the sisters in Louisiana who, when celebrating the parish's centenary, collaborated to publish in a brochure the names of all the individual priests who had served in the parish, while lumping all the sisters under a generic title. Or the sister in New York who, when asked by a fifth-grader if God loved boys more than girls, did not have an answer. "What the sisters taught me in school was what influenced me more than my parents," observed an Italian woman. "My mother was widowed early and was strong, not submissive. Being submissive came from the sisters."[13]

Women have so internalized the message of patriarchy that their behavior proclaims to everyone that they are "unworthy," that they have not been healed. They are a model that contradicts the message of Jesus for women.

Another message the patriarchal church imparts that many women have internalized is that of complementarity. How many times have women heard their role in the church defined as different but complementary? In Pope John Paul II's letter to women in July 1995, he said, "Woman complements man, just as man complements woman: Men and women are complementary. Womanhood expresses the 'human' as much as manhood does, but in a different and complementary way."[14]

Tom Fox explains the church's position on "complementarity" as:

> The church teaches that women are equal to men but by nature are different. The Creator intended that they "complement" men. Thus, their nature is different from men—and only men can "image" Jesus and officiate in the celebration of the Eucharist following Jesus' command: "Do this in memory of me."[15]

Clearly the institutional church places a strong emphasis on equality between women and men being understood as complementarity, not mutuality. When the church speaks of men and women in complementary roles, the male is always dominant and overshadows the female, who must assume a secondary role. Unfortunately, many women have accepted this flawed message of complementary roles for them in the church.

11

How then has it been possible for the strong feminist movement we experience to evolve in the church today? Two factors have greatly impacted this movement, namely, the enormous increase in the number of women studying theology and the birth of independent Catholic movements.

In the 1940s and '50s women for the first time gained access to formal theological education in this country. . . . Between 1976 and 1986, the total enrollment of women in programs leading to ordination (usually the Master of Divinity) rose 110 percent, whereas total seminary enrollment rose only 31 percent. Overall, the number of women eligible for ordination increased 219 percent during this time, whereas the number of eligible men rose by only 7.8 percent. By 1986 the number of women studying theology had more than quadrupled.[16] Since 1986 much of the growth in the Master of Divinity enrollment has come from an increase in female students. The number of women enrolled in Master of Divinity programs has increased from 25.7% in 1992 to 28.6% in 1996. Over the five years, the female enrollment has grown by 15.2% while male enrollment has actually declined by 0.7%.[17]

Rosemary Ruether maintains:

The last 30 years has spawned an enormous number of semiautonomous Catholic movements which continue to produce all kinds of communications that are not controlled by the hierarchy, i.e. the *National Catholic Reporter.* It is alternative news on the church that they don't get from mainline media.[18]

These alternate news sources, women theologians, writers, and lecturers, along with movements like Call to Action, Association for the Rights of Catholics in the Church, Women's Ordination Conference, and Future Church, are raising peoples' awareness to the debilitating effects of the hierarchical church, particularly on women. They are also reforming women's thinking and self-image in a manner that is enabling some to believe they are worthy. These movements are infusing fresh air into the church, producing oxygen that is life-giving for women and men alike.

NOTES

1. Miriam Therese Winter, Adair Lummis, and Allison Stokes, *Defecting in Place* (New York: Crossroad, 1994), 10.
2. Susan Muto, interview, April 1994.
3. Rosemary Radford Ruether, interview, March 1994.

4. Joan Chittister, interview, April 1994.

5. Ibid.

6. Bishop P. Francis Murphy, "Let's Start Over," *Commonweal,* 25 September 1992, 13.

7. Reuther, interview.

8. Elizabeth Schüssler Fiorenza, *Discipleship of Equals* (New York: Crossroad, 1993), 213.

9. Elizabeth Dodson Gray, *Patriarchy as a Conceptual Trap* (Wellesley, Mass.: Roundtable Press, 1982), 22.

10. Ruth McDonough Fitzpatrick, interview, March 1994.

11. Gerda Lerner, *The Creation of Patriarchy* (New York: Oxford University Press, 1986), 217.

12. Anne E. Carr, *Transforming Grace* (San Francisco: Harper & Row, 1988), 138–39.

13. Interview, woman from the Midwest.

14. Pope John Paul II. "Letter to Women" in *The Tablet, the International Catholic Weekly* (London, England, 15 July 1995): 918.

15. Thomas C. Fox, *Sexuality and Catholicism* (New York: George Braziller, 1995): 202.

16. Catherine Mowry La Cugna, "Catholic Women as Ministers and Theologians," *America* 167, no. 10 (10 October 1992): 239–40.

17. Johathan Strom and Daniel Aleshire, eds. *The Fact Book on Theological Education* (Pittsburgh, Penn.: The Association of Theological Schools, 1996–97), 45.

18. Ruether, interview.

Chapter 2

STANDING WITH THE TIDE

I think the greatest tragedy is that it is women who largely support the sexist system in Christianity, and that they are also misogynist. There is a great deal to be done to free women's spirits and minds.[1]

A discussion of women's cooperation in the patriarchal institutional church was brought to an abrupt halt when the women heard one of their group announce, "anyone who remains in the church and does not make waves stands with the tide of clerical oppression." These women had never thought of themselves as part of the "system."

All of us who attend Mass on Sunday and are participants in or witnesses to sexist language in hymns and liturgical prayer, the exclusion of women from major ministries, ill-prepared or oppressive homilies, or domineering clerical behavior are indeed collaborators in the patriarchal dominance of the church. Women who say, "those little things don't bother me," or "father doesn't mean anything by his language," or "father is elderly, we have to be patient and tolerant," are in fact prime examples of those who have been co-opted by the system. Others who grumble and complain on the way out of church but do not have the courage to confront father's behavior are also promoting its continuance. We laity, observed a woman from the Midwest, have all been so indoctrinated into this system that we are very reluctant to critique it. We shy away from saying it is "wrong" and settle for "unfair." Then we do not feel so challenged to do something about it.

Why do women do this? Why do so many make excuses, tolerate, and even embrace the very system that ignores their gifts and demeans their status as equal human beings?

One reason is the conditioning of women described in chapter one. Many women are truly convinced that it is God's will that women remain in "their place" in the church. They believe it because they have been indoctrinated by those clergy who interpret Scripture and tradition as justifying women's passive and submissive roles. They have accepted what patriarchy has taught them, namely, that they are subordinate, inferior, and sources of temptation, and that they do not image Christ and are therefore incapable of performing the ministries reserved to men. They also trust in what they believe to be superior male authority, which reinforces patterns of dependency, thus keeping them in a state of perpetual subordination.

Women who have internalized this message may accept a seat on the parish council but they rarely speak up. Rather, they often ask their husbands or male colleagues to present their ideas while they sit demurely at the table. Often women think loyalty to the church means that they cannot disagree with anything the church says or does. They presume that being faithful means their minds and intellects must be silenced. For some, this brings peace because they do not have to think. For others, it means living with the tension of being unauthentic.

One very effective means used by the church to convince women of their God-given role throughout the centuries has been the portrayal of Mary, the mother of Jesus, as a submissive, passive, obedient model for all women. Mary's courage, strength, and priestly role have been buried for centuries in the recesses of the patriarchal mind. Women who have embraced this deception would not think of asserting themselves or moving out of their prescribed role in the church.

This mentality causes women to devalue themselves and other women as well. If women feel unworthy to perform certain ministries in the church, often they will not approve of other women doing so. Such women thereby defend their heartfelt conviction against attack by those who in their view appear to be the enemy, namely, Catholic feminists. Although victimized by patriarchy, many women, in good faith, continue to support the system and help to perpetuate it.

These are the women who insist:

— the status quo for women is permanently ordained by God;
— women are not really "Catholic" if they don't obey the priest, the bishop, or the pope;
— women must accept the "infallible" declaration prohibiting women's ordination.

Their acceptance includes:

— emphasizing the "male" call to priesthood;
— affirming women's role to be equal but different;
— accepting a subordinate role to men in decision making;

— participating in the hierarchical management mode;
— dismissing alternative beliefs about women's role as wrong or heretical;
— using their power and influence to prevent change from happening in the parish.

Two reasons women embrace the patriarchal system are fear of change and loss of security. Women fear losing what they have as "good women" in the church and often do not have the vision to see that something far better could and must come about. As one woman from a midwestern city said:

> We'd like to think that we cherish diversity but when it comes down to the practice of it we're afraid of what that might mean. We can't let go of the flower we have in order to let something else bloom.

Some of these women are comfortable and secure with their status in the church, while others would like to change, but cannot bring themselves to do so. They feel to be submissive is the way one must act in order to be a good woman. "To change their status in any way is threatening to womanhood in general and to their womanhood in particular. They feel threatened and fear they will lose a whole way of life."[2] "Some like things the way they are, with women on a pedestal, getting small privileges," observed a sister from the West, "but you cannot have it both ways, being privileged and being equal." These same women are happy and feel honored to be able to do the small services women have always done. They like it when father smiles at them and says, "well done." They are grateful for any little crumb that is tossed to them by the clergy and they are afraid to risk losing it by seeking more.

One example of this was a group of women from a parish in the East, who participated in liturgy at a nearby monastery. When some wanted to ask for a more active role, the others said, "No, they are good men, they let us in. If you push they will close the door." In other words, do not rock the boat, let us be happy with these crumbs from the table.

Such women refuse to accept that all people in the church should be breaking bread together and no one should have to grovel for crumbs. Their actions oppress not only themselves but all women. They reinforce the message of patriarchy that women are second-class. "The women who feel this way come out of a whole bundle of stereotypes of what women must be, should be, ought to be, and if they break that stereotype, they are really in trouble," says Miriam Therese Winter.[3]

Women who stand with the clergy fear not only change and the insecurity it brings but also fear women who are struggling to bring patriarchy to its knees. They are suspicious of articulate, assertive women who strive for co-discipleship for two reasons: either they equate their agenda with the secular feminist agenda, or they are afraid of the feelings that female role models might awaken in them. Both are motivations to cling even more tenaciously to the security of the patriarchal system.

A group of women theologians and students in a large midwestern city provided some insights into these fears and the resulting behavior:

> I think that women who assume leadership roles are sometimes opposed by their peers because they are not used to seeing women in a leadership role. They are threatened. They've never done it themselves and don't want to get pushed into it. I don't want that role model held up for me. [Student]

> It's very threatening for a woman who wants to stay where she is in the church to see another woman doing something different. [Theologian]

> I think women also fear success because if I go to the front of the bus and start driving, I'm responsible for everybody behind me. I realize they are following me and I'm not always comfortable with that. [Student]

The more frightened women are, the angrier they are with women who promote equality. They try to keep the church "right" and do not want other women destroying that place where they find certainty and security. Women who have constructed their identity within the patriarchal system, who feel that God as "father" means everything important to them, are repulsed by the mere suggestion that they pray to God as "mother." They find feminist theology threatening because it requires reconstructing their entire identity if they are to embrace it. It is a threat to their very selfhood.[4]

Within that group of articulate, assertive women, sisters are often singled out for criticism and attack, even though many have made great contributions, particularly in the fields of education and health care. As a group they have been well educated and have held leadership roles in church-sponsored institutions. Mary Collins, OSB, suggests that there is a fear of women religious, and the anxiety probably comes out of a historical system in the church that set various groups of women against one another, and, in fact, ranked their worth. Women in religious congregations, she noted, appear to other women as a natural enemy.[5] Sisters have been privileged and placed on pedestals in the church for centuries, forming an elite group that left women in the pews with a sense of inferiority. (See chapter 5.)

Another category of women have simply "shut down." They avoid reading any new theology and refuse to attend lectures that might raise their awareness to the evils of patriarchy. Because of their own insecurity they resist exposing themselves to anything that might change their minds about women's place in the church. They fear freedom from patriarchal oppression because of the consequences. If women were to raise their awareness they might be compelled to speak out against sexism in the church, might refuse to contribute to an oppressive bishop or pastor, or might even go so far as to participate in boycotts or picketing. They would ultimately run the risk of losing favor with the clergy, having their female friends back away, becoming ostracized in their parish, and losing their image as "good Catholic women." For many, the price is too great.

When urged by others to work for change in the church such women offer the rationale that they are really "better off" than their mothers and grandmothers. This is usually accompanied by such remarks as, "progress for women just takes time," or "look at all the changes that have come about since Vatican II, just be patient and it will happen." The remark that enrages Catholic feminists most is, "If it's God's will it will happen!" Women who have been co-opted into the system defend their behavior by declaring that changes are happening anyway. They ask, "why rock the boat?"

Often women are more interested in keeping up their image of the "good Catholic woman" than in challenging the injustices of the status quo. Some truly believe they can do more good for women by not making waves, by showing through their example that women are capable of ministering peacefully within the church structure. What they do not understand is that by not making waves they are endorsing patriarchy and keeping the door to equality closed.

Ultimately, the issue is "price." What are women willing to pay for equality in their church? As Regina Coll, CSJ, observes,

> To invite women into feminism is to invite them into a very painful place. They can't read the Bible the same way, they can't go to Mass the same way and they can't read the *New York Times* the same way. Everything is different. Everything is changed once they have that conversion and it's painful and wonderful at the same time. Those who do not enter in are held back by a deep sense that they are going to lose more than they are going to gain. [6]

Sisters and other women who have always been favored by the pastor or bishop perceive that they have benefited a great deal. What they have received may be only a pittance, but they know it is more than they would get if they assumed a critical stance.

> We get really excited when a priest smiles and says, "good job," or any little crumb that's tossed to women. Sometimes when you are raised up to be president of the cookie club, it's taken as an honor when you should be given the opportunity to be president of the parish council.[7]

These women do not want to lose their benefits, their place, their favor with those in power. The price is simply too high.

Joan Chittister noted that after reading letters from hundreds of women, she realized yet again "that to be a woman in a man's church demands a price too high for growing numbers to pay." Her reaction was, "this is tragic, really tragic."[8]

Elizabeth Johnson, CSJ, observes that, "if you are too much of a feminist you will not last in a parish or diocesan structure. There is a tension because you have to work within the limits of the system. In a parish or diocese you are paid to keep the ball rolling, so if you become too critical or allow yourself to become involved in full-scale criticism of patriarchy, you are not going to last. The cost of discipleship, of speaking out against the injustices of the church, is often your job. For many women this is too great a price."[9]

When women become aware of the injustices perpetrated on them by the church they often become aware of injustice in all aspects of their lives: personal, professional, and social. When women begin to speak up against their treatment as second-class citizens by the clergy, many soon realize that they have to examine all of their relationships. How can they fight for equality in the church and accept less in their marriages or, in the case of sisters, refuse to examine the effects of their religious formation? The consequences are costly indeed.

Too many women today persistently stand with the tide of clerical oppression, for several reasons: because they continue to benefit from it, they are too fearful to challenge it, or they do not understand the connection between their formation and their behavior. Some women who accompanied their husbands in preparation for the deaconate were interviewed and shared their experiences. In one instance, the priest conducting the class told the women they should remember that it was their husbands who were important and not they! All of them kept silent, took his abuse, and "offered it up" so that their husbands could be ordained. None of them would admit that the price was too high, and they could not acknowledge that their behavior contributed to the oppression of women.

If women repress or deny the violence of the church, either by their silence or by their refusal to act against it, it may be that, according to Elizabeth Schüssler Fiorenza, they are behaving like battered women, fearfully remaining in a violent home situation.[10] They do not believe in the possibility of change and the power of God's grace.

At ninety, Mary Luke Tobin, SL, is still preaching the message she heard at Vatican II, where she was empowered by a statement in the document on the Church in the Modern World:

> Every type of discrimination, whether social or cultural, whether based on sex, race, color, social condition, language or religion, is to be overcome and eradicated as contrary to God's intent. For in truth it must still be regretted that fundamental personal rights are not yet being universally honored. Such is the case of a woman who is denied the right and freedom to choose a husband, to embrace a state of life, or to acquire an education or cultural benefits equal to those recognized for men.[11]

Tobin asks, "What do these words really mean to the bishops?" I see them cowering in the corner, unequal to the kind of change demanded of them. Shaking her finger, she says,

> I want to say, "brothers, you don't have to cower back there. Come out and be who you are, free human persons in the church and insist on that for women also." Until they do that, women have this uphill battle, because too many buy into the patriarchal system. *The very thing these women are promoting is going to be the dagger in our backs and will keep us from rising.*[12]

NOTES

1. Miriam Therese Winter, Adair Lummis, and Allison Stokes, *Defecting in Place* (New York: Crossroad, 1994), 24.
2. Miriam Therese Winter, interview, March 1994.
3. Ibid.
4. Elizabeth A. Johnson, CSJ, interview, April 1994.
5. Mary Collins, OSB, interview, March 1994.
6. Regina Coll, CSJ, interview, February 1994.
7. Winter, interview.
8. Joan Chittister, "Police Protect Church from Onslaught of Women Praying for Church Justice," *National Catholic Reporter,* 23 December 1994, 9.
9. Elizabeth Johnson, CSJ, interview, April 1994.
10. Elizabeth Schüssler Fiorenza, *Discipleship of Equals* (New York: Crossroad, 1993), 248.
11. Walter M. Abbott, ed., "Pastoral Constitution on the Church in the Modern World," *The Documents of Vatican II* (New York: America Press, 1966), 227–28.
12. Mary Luke Tobin, SL, interview, March 1994.

Chapter 3

THE POWER PARADIGM

The tradition of female submission and subordination holds on like a long bitter winter, even though the calendar marks the coming of spring[1]

Understanding the use of power is critical to effecting change in the church. It is much easier to say we believe in equal roles for women than it is to actively insist that women be allowed to preach. As long as women give lip service to principles but are unwilling to act, the effect is like running in place: they work up a lot of sweat, but get nowhere. Women will remain strangers and even enemies until they find ways of joining together to resist the concepts, values, and structures that promote the two-tiered system created by the hierarchical church. Then, and only then, will women move from sporadic attempts to "balance" or "equalize" the hierarchy to efforts at transforming its monolithic ordering of the church.

By restricting the priesthood, and therefore all positions of power, to men, the Vatican clearly suggests that women do not and should not have power of any dimension. Additionally, the hierarchy fosters the notion that women do not need power. Their rationale is often provided through tradition and scriptural interpretations.

> For example, John Paul II maintains that if Christ—by His free and sovereign choice, clearly attested to by the Gospel and by the Church's constant tradition—entrusted only to men the task of being an "icon" of His countenance as "shepherd" and "bridegroom" of the Church through the exercise of the ministerial priesthood, this in no way detracts from the role of women. . . . [2]

But what do women themselves think about power? How do they understand it? Do Catholic women accept the premise that the source of all power is God and that God's power is not power over but power with? Too often power is associated only with ordination, and women forget about the power inherent in baptism, the power to share in the priesthood of Christ in his prophetic and royal mission. Jeanette Sherrill, in *Power and Authority,* contends:

> Our power is not power that has been granted by some external source or institution, it is a power that comes from within as we are empowered by God. Jesus' power was drawn from his relationship with God. Such power is different from the power of authority which may also be granted by an external source or institution.[3]

The question remains, how are women empowered by God in this church? By restricting power to men alone, does the church infer women are incapable of having the same relationship with God as men and therefore, cannot be empowered? The institutional church, by reserving to itself the right to decide who are the recipients of priestly power, is denying the fact that we are all empowered by God through baptism.

There are many unanswered questions regarding women's use of power, particularly in regard to the dynamics of female relationships that cause some women to oppress and even attack powerful women. Perhaps many women are envious of women who have attained positions of power. Conceivably, they do not trust them because they fear how strong women might use or misuse their power.

Such reflections pose the question: If mainstream Catholic women fear such misuse of power, is it precisely that fear that keeps them from uniting?

Such comments as "we don't recognize power even when we have it," "we don't associate our work with an expression of power," or "we have not seriously studied power, so we don't know how to practice it except as it is," seem to indicate either an ignorance of the value of power for women or a fearful reluctance to address the underlying cause of their own oppression.

If women want to bring about change in the ways in which power is understood and used, "they must be self-consciously intentional in this task. It is a teaching task as well as a modeling task if new power relationships are to be permanent."[4] The task is to move women beyond the fear of admitting they want or need power to an understanding that without it they cannot successfully effect any type of change.

Hedrick Smith maintains, "Power is the mysterious quotient, the ability to make something happen or to keep it from happening."[5] The hierarchy understands well the enigma of power. Smith also suggests that women seldom seize the opportunity to employ the intangible ingredients that constitute power:

24

Information and knowledge are power. Visibility is power. A sense of timing is power. Trust and integrity are power. Personal energy is power; so is self-confidence. Access to the inner sanctum is power. Obstruction and delay are power. Winning is power. Sometimes the illusion of power is power.[6]

When women do try to use their power, they often emulate the behavior of their male counterparts, resulting in the oppression of other women. Is it, as Doris Donnelly suggests, "that somebody's got to be on top?"[7]

Richard Rohr contends that in the patriarchal view all relationships are eventually defined in terms of superiority and inferiority, and the all-important need for order and control is assured by the exercise of dominative power.[8] For the one who happens to be on top, the system is perceived as working well. It certainly makes for good order, especially for those on top.

Perhaps, as Doris Donnelly suggests, some women, especially those in positions of authority, do not know how to use power because they do not have mentors and they do not see many people using it well. "So much of our experience of power is negative. The misuse of power dehumanizes. What we need are positive models so that we can see a different way the game can be played."[9]

The tragedy, she says, is that when some women seize power they seize it for the same wrong reasons that men do. "It is a gradual thing, you sniff it, you desire it, you lust for it. And so help me, when you do get it you're going to do the same to others. And women perpetuate the same thing."[10]

One of the reasons why women buy into patriarchy, observed one sister, is because of enculturation and because they'd like a piece of the action, a piece of the power. If they've been stepped on all along and can get a little power, it feels good.

When women assume power, they often duplicate the patriarchal model and use their power against other women, since it is the only model they know. Women frequently experienced this kind of power in women principals and administrators who operated in a "man's world" before Vatican II. More will be said about this in chapter five. Simply including women as part of the male power base is not the answer. The power base must be changed, and inclusive models need to be introduced that exchange dominance and submission for teamwork and collaboration as the two hinges on which power swings.

Power in any form has come slowly to a small number of United States Catholic women. Some are repelled by how it is used and often misused by men, while others actively seek to imitate their male counterparts and covet power, without hesitating to wield authority over other women. However, most mainstream Catholic women do not desire or pursue power in the church. For them, the church is where they go to pray, to gain strength and consolation, and to receive the sacraments. Nonetheless, there are some women who use power well, without manipulation, authentically challenging others and thereby freeing them to respond.

Although sociological and psychological studies have been conducted to determine why women do not seek or use power in society, far less is documented concerning mainstream Catholic women's use and abuse of power.[11] The tradition of female submission and subordination in the church is multifaceted and complex. Understanding the role women play in perpetuating their own oppression will raise awareness and hopefully effect change.

It is a mistake to presume that women's marginalization has united them and provided a support system for other women. What Susan Muto experienced in her association with women through the years was a deep level of disappointment. At those points in her life when she most needed other women, she found herself abandoned. Women withdrew support.[12] Understanding patriarchal structures and how they affect women helps us comprehend the behavior Muto describes.

Elizabeth Dodson Gray's description of the conceptual trap of patriarchy offers some clarity to our understanding of why Catholic women cannot envision any other model.

> A conceptual trap is to the thought world of the mind what the astronomer's black holes are to the universe. Once inside, there seems to be no way of getting out or seeing out. A conceptual trap is a way of thinking that is like a room which—once inside—you cannot imagine a world outside.[13]

Such thinking controls our understanding of power and authority, and therefore affects our relationships. If, as Gerda Lerner maintains in her book *The Creation of Patriarchy*, patriarchy can only function with the cooperation of women, then understanding women's participation in the process of their own oppression is crucial.

The Catholic church, like society, is grounded in a hierarchal structure where women are perceived to be inferior and are marginalized. The language of marginalization in the church reinforces the systemic devaluation of women.

> Women are valued less than men, they do not have as much importance. Marginal also means the effacing of women, for women are not men, and hence are not really present and can be overlooked; in this sense marginal means having no substance, containing nothing, the emptiness of the margins. Marginal implies also the notion of borderline or limit or edge, as a margin defines the

edge of a text. Here women are cast as the border—literally the margin—which demarcates order and chaos. As the border of the social-symbolic order women take on characteristics of the chaos so feared by the order.[14]

In this context, women are neither inside nor outside, neither known nor unknown. It is this position that has enabled male cultures, such as the hierarchy of the church, at times to vilify women as representing darkness and chaos. Operating from this position of ambiguity and uncertainty encourages the divisiveness that perpetuates the hierarchal infrastructure of the church rather than promoting the equality and solidarity of women.

Rosemary Radford Ruether suggests that the clergy have been seen as an ecclesiastical counterpart of the power of the father in the family. At the same time, women have been excluded both from the ordained clergy and [in the past] from access to higher theological education and from the teaching of theology.[15] The church, she says, has not only modeled itself after the patriarchal social hierarchy, but has also acted as the ultimate ideological sanction for this system, naming it both in its ecclesiastical and its social forms as expressions of the will of God and the order of creation.[16]

For women who are continually marginalized in the church, this is especially problematical. It is very hard for oppressed people to organize because of divisive tendencies. The disagreement among women's groups and their inability to come together agreeably was illustrated at the Women Church Conference in Albuquerque, New Mexico, in 1993. Many women attended with the hope and expectation of being a part of a group of over three thousand women who were gathering for the same reason—and they were very wrong. It seemed every group had its own agenda and, at the end of the three days, there was great divisiveness, hostility, suspicion, and jealousy; real oppression; and more separateness, exemplifying the female face of patriarchy. As one woman sagely remarked, "If this is what the church of the future is going to be, count me out!"

Two years later, indications of divisiveness among women working for equality in the church were again exhibited at the Women's Ordination Conference Gathering 95. Tom Fox, editor of the *National Catholic Reporter*, observed:

> During the Gathering, evidence of a long-simmering internal split within the membership emerged for the first time in public view. The basic division was whether the organization should continue to seek ordination in the Roman Catholic Church. Those arguing against ordination stated that Catholicism is inherently patriarchal and that by entering the clerical ranks, women would perpetuate church injustices.[17]

Fox indicated that the faction arguing against ordination was led by theologian Elizabeth Schüssler Fiorenza. Others, led by Maureen Fiedler, SL, and Jeannine Gramick, SSND, made it clear they still advocated women's ordination though in reformed church structures.

Examples of divisiveness among women struggling for equality are not peculiar to this century. As far back as 1886, Elizabeth Cady Stanton led a group who charged that the church was the greatest barrier to women's emancipation. Simultaneously, Susan B. Anthony countered that the debates about religion would divide the suffragists and consistently tried to table discussions about the controversial resolutions proposed by Stanton and her counterparts. It was over the issue of religion that Stanton's radicalism came most into conflict with Anthony's political pragmatism.[18]

Rosemary Radford Ruether suggests that if you do not internalize your own ways to divide and conquer, the system will go out and find ways to do it for you. She contends that frequently women chart their own course, not bonding with others, creating fragmentation and inhibiting solidarity. Women often hesitate to discuss their situation or even imagine something different because the patriarchal culture obscures reality.

> Women in general have very low self-esteem and grow up thinking they are second class. When a woman is successful, there's this voice in the back of her head that says, "any minute I can fail. I made it this time, but . . . "[19]

> Women have been conditioned so much that we don't even know we are supporting the hierarchy. We are told that our opinions aren't worth anything and we tell each other the same thing. We don't affirm each other. [Married Woman, Illinois]

In order to dispel the unconsciousness that keeps them inert, women must confront their reality. Women will move toward liberation when they become aware of how some of the hierarchy are controlling them. Then they will be able to break those bonds and unite. Ruether's aim is to support women in overcoming the internalization of subjugation so that they may network, organize, and create some of that change in both church and the larger society.[20] This will be achieved through education, alerting women to the consequences of their acceptance of teachings and clerical support oppressive to women.

The capacity to oppress is not a male characteristic. It is a power characteristic. As women have demonstrated, they are just as capable of it as men. As a woman in the southeast indicated, "You can find oppressive, hit-you-below-the-belt women as well as men in the church."[21]

We have become so conditioned to suspect the use of power, however, that even when women exercise power in positive ways it is often rejected. A sister in a southern parish who began to preach at the invitation of the priest spoke of losing the support of many women because she dared to assume a traditionally male role. They resented it and were angry. Another sister from the same area told of women in her parish who, instead of supporting her, "checked out" everything she said and did with "father." Several women interviewed admitted to oppressing other women because they were moving outside acceptable women's roles. The women felt that a man should do the job and it was embarrassing for a woman to do it. They acknowledged that sometimes they even worked to have a man get the job.

> Sometimes women don't feel comfortable doing a job and can't understand how another woman can. It's less an objection than a lack of understanding. They say, "You shouldn't be there," as opposed to "why are you there?" [Single Woman, California]

Sandra Schneiders asserts that women who associate themselves with the male power structure often do not want other women on a par with themselves. Because women are reluctant to come together and are uncomfortable exercising power in ways advantageous to their gender, solidarity is minimal.

> There are women who love to be oppressed by men and can't stand it if women are their equals. Once women make it in a men's system they prefer to be approved by men rather than be in colleagueship or sisterhood with women whom the men see as inferior.[22]

At the end of the twentieth century, women remain divided regarding their feelings about their limited opportunities for full and equal participation in church life. Many remain reluctant to acknowledge that until women claim their own power they cannot successfully effect any type of change.

As many continue to wait for the coming of spring and the hope of new life for women in the church, many other submissive and subordinate women hold on to the long bitter winter of patriarchal oppression.

NOTES

1. Sherrye Henry, *The Deep Divide: Why American Women Resist Equality* (New York: Macmillan Publishing Company, 1994), 212.

2. Pope John Paul II's "A Letter to Women," dated 29 June and released 10 July 1995 at the Vatican.

3. Jeanette R. Sherrill, *Power and Authority: Issues for Women Clergy as Leaders* (New York: Hartford Seminary, 1991), 25–26.

4. Ibid., 45.

5. Hedrick Smith, *The Power Game: How Washington Works* (New York: Random House, 1988), xxi–xxii.

6. Ibid., 42.

7. Doris Donnelly, interview, April 1994.

8. Richard Rohr, *Simplicity: the Art of Living* (New York: Crossroad, 1991), 124–25.

9. Doris Donnelly, interview, April 1994.

10. Ibid.

11. Thomas E. Wartenberg, *The Forms of Power: From Domination to Transformation* (Philadelphia: Temple University Press, 1990); J. B. Miller, "Psychoanalysis, Patriarchy and Power: One Viewpoint on Women's Goals and Needs," *Chrysalis* 2 (1977): 19–25.

12. Susan Muto, interview, April 1994.

13. Elizabeth Dodson Gray, *Patriarchy as a Conceptual Trap* (Wellesley, Mass.: Roundtable Press, 1982), 17.

14. Rebecca S. Chopp, introduction to *The Power to Speak: Feminism, Language, God* (New York: Crossroad, 1989).

15. Rosemary Radford Ruether, "Sexism as Ideology and Social System: Can Christianity Be Liberated from Patriarchy?" in *With Both Eyes Open: Seeing Beyond Gender,* Patricia Altenbernd Johnson and Janet Kalven, eds. (New York: Pilgrim Press, 1988), 148–49.

16. Ibid., 153.; see also Pope John Paul II, "A Letter to Women." in *The Tablet, the International Catholic Weekly* (London, England: 15 July 1995): 917–19.

17. Tom Fox, ed., *National Catholic Reporter,* Kansas City, Mo., 32, no. 10 (29 December 1995/5 January 1996): 5. See also John Paul II's "A letter to Women," July, 1995.

18. Maureen Fitzgerald, forward to *The Woman's Bible,* by Elizabeth Cady Stanton (Boston: Northeastern University Press, 1993), xxiii–xxiv.

19. Joyce Rupp, OSM, interview, April 1994.

20. Rosemary Radford Ruether, interview, April 1994.

21. Miriam Therese Winter, Adair Lummis, and Allison Stokes, *Defecting in Place* (New York: Crossroad, 1994), 75.

22. Sandra Schneiders, interview, April 1994.

Chapter 4

MENTORS OR TORMENTORS?

The paradox is that the very thing women claim to be fighting in the male population is exactly what they are duplicating in the female population.[1]

Patriarchy is a tool used by the institutional church that constructs divisiveness among women. As chapter 2 illustrated, many women choose to stand on the side of patriarchy against women who are struggling for equality. Feminism, on the other hand, is an attempt to unite women against patriarchy but because so many women are co-opted into the system, it is also a wedge that is keeping women apart.

The very word "feminism" raises a red flag among some Catholic women today. Many do not distinguish between the agenda of the secular feminist movement and that of Catholic feminists. Therefore, they equate women who are struggling against patriarchy for co-discipleship in the church with women who are anti-male and/or pro-abortion. Since they cannot countenance the latter they refuse to even consider the agenda of the former.

The more traditional some Catholic women are, the more critical they seem to be of feminist Catholic women. These women are uncompromising in their interpretation of Scripture and rely heavily on the teaching authority of the pope. There is no such thing as a "casual" right-wing Catholic woman. They are convinced that there is only one way to be a Catholic and if you do not agree with their way, they will strive to "convert" you. The pope's strong pronouncements against birth control and women's ordination, along with the Vatican's rejection of inclusive language for the *Catechism of the Catholic Church*, the *Sacramentary,* and the Scriptures, strengthen their belief in the righteousness of their cause against more liberal Catholic women.

When interviewed, Susan Muto related her experience of trying to discuss the various drafts of the Bishops' Pastoral on Women with female representatives from the far right and the far left. The far right, she noted, not only hated the far left but refused to engage in respectful dialogue. They could not imagine that someone on the other side might have an idea worthy of consideration. Why not search for the truth? The truth will make us free. None of us has complete access to any truth. She pointed out that not only a lack of courtesy and politeness, but also hatred and sometimes rage prevailed among the women.

> I would see women from different camps walk into these meetings and literally stand up and leave not even agreeing to disagree agreeably. . . . The genius of womanhood ought to be to sit and talk.[2]

Muto questioned: What is the matter with women? What is it that makes it so difficult for them to move off of dead center? Why does one group feel that it will only be happy if it puts the other group down? Why does it have to be this way? Her conclusion was that women have to do a lot of soul-searching about these questions. By no means does Muto mean to imply that it is only women who behave in this manner. "The paradox," she observes, "is that the very thing they claim to be fighting in the male population is exactly what women are duplicating in the female population."

Because the Catholic Church has never been a monolithic community of believers, we should not be surprised that women adhere to different factions within the church. Some women are adversarial because they perceive they have much to lose. The stability that was theirs as Catholics prior to Vatican II is threatened by a more open interpretation of the Scriptures and of church doctrine.

Men may be afraid of losing their power and prestige if women achieve equality, but some women are even more afraid of losing their status, inferior as it is. If women end up in a worse state, they are going to be very angry at the women who effect change. Because women often do not trust themselves, they do not trust other women. Often it is unclear who the real enemy is. What is sadly revealing is that rigid fidelity to either liberal or conservative Catholicism, when it takes precedence over the message of Jesus to love one another, results in fear.

Some women, because of their formation, are unable to participate in the conflict with patriarchy. They have internalized the belief that the patriarchal system is the will of God. In addition, there are a vast number of middle-of-the-road women, who are oblivious or who choose not to become involved in the struggle. These are the "good women" and "good sisters," described in chapter 2, some of whom opt not to become involved, while others have not yet awakened and stand with the tide of clerical oppression, choosing not to make waves.

Examples from across the United States of women acting as tormentors to other women illustrate the fact that this behavior is not only very real but also extremely common.

I have met and worked with women who demean my working on women's issues in the church. [Married Woman, Wisconsin]

As I witnessed the formation of the first women's commission in the Chicago archdiocese in 1993, I have been saddened by how the members are unable to work together and how divisive the group has been between liberals and conservatives, including *Opus Dei*. [3] By undercutting their own organization, they are giving people fuel for the fire to say, "Women can't accomplish anything." [Sister, Illinois]

A woman came up to me when I was distributing communion, pushed my hand away, and said, "I want father." [Older Woman, Ohio]

While demonstrating for women's ordination, I found the faces of the women who were watching far more aggressive than the men's. There were looks of disdain and hatred. We threatened something secure and comfortable that they don't want changed. [Married Woman, Washington, D.C.]

We have a support group for all women who work for the church. We share our experiences of being told we are crazy, idealistic, strange, bad, emotional, etc., by priests and other women. [Young Married Woman, Illinois]

I had been leading a women's prayer group over several weeks when one woman said, "Wouldn't it be great if father could come once in awhile and lead our group?" [Sister, California]

A Hispanic woman who started being a eucharistic minister was confronted by the women in her family, "What are you trying to do, buy your way into heaven?" They didn't want that model held up because they were afraid to do it themselves. [Young Widow, Indiana]

A sister who began a prayer with, "In the name of the Creator," was accosted by a woman. "Who do you think you are? Why aren't you wearing a habit?" She then proceeded to write to the bishop about her. [Sister, Pennsylvania]

I feel that women who think the organization of the church is divinely ordained, that it came directly from God are an obstacle to those of us working for the recognition of equality of women and men in the church. [Sister, Colorado]

Women in my parish tried to shame me for not following the pope, for not respecting the archbishop and not having a supportive demeanor. They gave me the silent treatment. Their attitude is that only men are worthy. [Single Woman, Texas]

Within these groups of women is a hierarchy of power and submission that flows from the divisive conditioning of patriarchal dominance. Some sisters feel they have come far in the church and that other women should have to pay a price to be accepted by them. Other women experience a sense of inferiority. "I felt, on more than one occasion, a kind of elitism among the sisters; an attitude of, 'you are a layperson and we are nuns, what could you possibly have to teach us?'"[4]

Married women are often the ones who organize the parish activities, set the agenda, line up the ministries, and exclude as much as possible the single, divorced, or separated women who might be a threat to them. Single women, in whatever category, expressed feelings of prejudice and suspicion from married women and sisters: "A married women's network runs the parish. We single women can't get in and there is no effort to include us."[5] Susan Muto notes:

As women, we have to own that sinful part of us and begin to work with it. Perhaps that sinful part of us is all mixed up with feelings of almost a mythological, allegorical sense of not being respected sufficiently by our male counterparts.[6]

The role of tormentor is easy to assume. To avoid becoming prey to it, women have to make a conscious effort, wherever they are and whenever they can, to lift one another up; to be inclusive; to level the barriers that divide them; to be aware of their dark side; and to be very careful that they do not do to others what they have had done to them.

In addition to women in parish and diocesan situations, female tormentors can also be found among those who have, in a sense, "made it" in the church. Besides sisters, these include Episcopal women who are ordained priests and who emulate male clerics.

To believe that only women need emancipation implies that men are already freed. The objective then becomes for women to become as much like men as possible. If there is only one nature, and men are presumed to have had a better chance to develop humanly, then the best thing for women is to get a piece of the pie men have been enjoying for so long. Learn the tricks of surviving in the male system; beat them at their own game.[7]

An Anglican woman who had been a priest for ten years admitted she had been oppressive to women for most of her priesthood because she knew no other model than patriarchy. As Dody Donnelly notes, "Because these women feel compelled to fulfill a stereotype, they don't always do too well in their treatment of other women."[8] Many women within the Catholic Church who want to be involved in full ministry often exhibit oppressive behavior, causing other women to be fearful of ever being subject to them, should they achieve their goal.

> We don't need women in Roman collars and robes, titled, working to be bishop, cardinal, and politicizing to be pope. We need women filled with the Holy Spirit to be Jesus where they are.[9]

To envision authoritative, oppressive women priests or bishops is a frightening concept that most women resist. Mary Collins capsulized such concern when she noted that the voice of a woman who abuses authority can be just as overwhelming and oppressive as the voice of a man. [10]

On the other hand, it is well to remember that "women often take subjugation from men but are resistant to taking it from women," notes Doris Donnelly.[11] This may be due to long-term conditioning and also to the fact that there are too few women role models who use authority in a positive, feminist way. Out of a sense of loyalty to the clergy, women do not speak up. We have been trained to hold our peace, particularly in church situations. We choose our fights, where we want to put our energy. It's a matter of assuming responsibility and making decisions. "What I need are people around me who are handling decisions well. There are so few models of women who do that."[12]

One reason women have not experienced more creative feminine leadership is because women in leadership positions frequently adopt the same strategies that patriarchy uses to rid itself of feminism, namely: *trivialization* (the view that other problems are much more important); *particularization* (the feeling that this is just a Catholic problem); *spiritualization* (the refusal to look at the concrete oppressive facts); and *universalization*, (the view that the real problem is human liberation).[13]

Of these four, the one most often used by women is trivialization. When a woman poses questions regarding inclusive language, women deacons, co-decision-making, women priests, or the like, the response frequently is, "are you on the subject of women again, when there are so many more important problems facing us, like homelessness, pollution, and poverty?" One assumption is that there is no correlation between women's oppression and these issues. Another, more problematic, assumption is that trivialization is used as a coping mechanism to divert attention from issues too painful to discuss. These reactions often put a feminist on the defensive or, because of patriarchal conditioning, instill doubt, causing her to retreat. Female trivialization is a powerful tool in the hands of women oppressors.

There were many women across this country who spoke of their efforts to mentor other women. Their responses to the question, "Have you ever made a conscious effort to assist other women in their struggle for equality in the church," give a ray of hope:

I support those who wish to be ordained, help them realize they are in oppressive situations, and encourage them to own who they are and to speak out. [Middle-Aged Married Woman, Pennsylvania]

I support women seeking equality and ordination. I encourage them to become lectors, eucharistic ministers, and to join women's prayer groups. [Older Woman, Maryland]

A sister encouraged me and gave me opportunities to preside at para-liturgies and to do spiritual direction. [Middle-Aged Woman, Maryland]

I accept speaking engagements that will put me on the line so I can join in the struggle by supporting, listening, naming gifts, and empowering women. [Sister, New York]

I encouraged a woman who wants to be equal and who was treated very poorly by a priest. I also signed the ad to the bishop asking that they not affirm the women's pastoral. [Widow, California]

I support and encourage women who are willing to speak out. I also mentor lay leadership of women. [Sister, Illinois]

I am helping to develop a "unity commission" in our parish to look at inclusion/exclusion in the church. [Young Married Woman, Illinois]

I tell women not to wait for them to give you permission, do what you have to do. [Sister, California]

I support women in positions of leadership in our parish by becoming parish council president to give women a voice. I advocate women's representation on every committee. [Young Married Woman, California]

A woman in our parish called me by name to step out in the parish. She also called me by her example. [Young Single Woman, Illinois]

I encourage women to go for training and to risk challenging the clergy so they might be able to use their natural leadership abilities. [Middle-Aged Woman, Illinois]

These are the voices of women in parishes and dioceses; women who are homemakers, professionals, single and married, as well as vowed religious. Women theologians, teachers, speakers, and writers are also constantly striving to raise women's awareness to their own leadership gifts, as well as to their oppression in the church. However, as Elizabeth Johnson, CSJ, sagely observed, "There are not enough women mentors (of this mind-set) and the few there are can become too mentored out."[14]

The critical need for female mentors is evident to all women who struggle for codiscipleship. They are continually asking, "where are the mentors for women in the church? Where are the counselors, the guides, the gurus, the teachers, the tutors, the advisors, the advocates, the proponents, the supporters of women?" By and large, women's supporters are women, but there are also some men, among the clergy and otherwise, who struggle to promote the message of Jesus for women.

Unfortunately, there is also an abundance of well-intended but misdirected mentors. These are women who have so internalized the message of patriarchy that they believe they are truly helping women fulfill their God-given role in the church when they counsel and guide them to:

—believe that women's role is equal but different;
—accept the status quo;
—be patient because the church moves slowly;
—believe that the pope and the bishops are doing all they can for women;
—rejoice in all the things women can do at this time in the church.

These Catholic women would find it difficult, if not impossible, to see that what they envision as a support for women is, in fact, an act of oppression.

Many are devoted to keeping the church "right" because they cannot imagine any other way for the church. Most of these well-intentioned mentors are middle-class women who on some level know that the achievement of women's equality would mean that all aspects of their life would be jeopardized. The "good woman" in the church and the "good woman" at home would lose her identity. These women do not want other women destroying their world or their church, so they work hard at preserving both, often to their own detriment. Women are frequently manipulated by the very system they support, satisfied as second class, while counseling others to accept a view of themselves that not only is not Christian, but also is against what God has created women to be.[15]

Unless women's awareness is raised, and until they understand fully their own oppression, they will never help themselves or others. Paulo Friere has pointed out "that the process of liberation from oppression is . . . a process of coming to awareness of one's own oppression and beginning to take action to overcome that oppression."[16] The greatest challenge facing Catholic women today is to address the task of raising women's consciousness to the fact that they belong to an oppressed group and have suffered grave injustices. It is not God's will that they remain oppressed.

Gerda Lerner, in *The Creation of a Feminist Consciousness,* outlines four challenges to women applicable to society and the church:

1) women must recognize that their subordination is not natural, but societally [patriarchally] determined;
2) women must develop a sense of sisterhood, a support system;
3) women have to work together to define their goals and strategies for changing their condition;
4) women must develop an alternative vision of the future.[17]

This last challenge can be interpreted to mean that women must generate a new way of belonging to the church, in which their use of power will call forth mutuality and creative service rather than subjugation and oppression. In such a church more women will be empowered to agree to disagree agreeably. Elizabeth Schüssler Fiorenza describes this moment:

> As a "rainbow" discipleship of equals we can voice and celebrate our differences because we have as a "common ground" our commitment to the liberation struggle and vision of God's *basileia,* God's intended world and community of well-being for all.[18]

NOTES

1. Susan Muto, interview, April 1994.
2. Ibid.
3. Opus Dei (Latin, "work of God"). Religious movement founded by Msgr. Josemaría Escrivá de Balaguer (1902–75) in Spain. Begun as a pious association of laypeople (and clergy) dedicated to their sanctification and that of society.

    Taken from *The HarperCollins Encyclopedia of Catholicism,* Richard P. McBrien, ed. (San Francisco: HarperCollins Publishers, 1995), 934.
4. Muto, interview, April 1995.

5. Single woman, interview.

6. Muto, interview, April 1994.

7. Regina A. Coll, CSJ, *Christianity and Feminism in Conversation* (Mystic, Conn.: Twenty-Third Publications, 1994), 80.

8. Dody Donnelly, interview, February 1994.

9. Miriam Therese Winter, Adair Lummis, and Allison Stokes, *Defecting in Place* (New York: Crossroad, 1994), 21.

10. Mary Collins, interview, March 1994.

11. Doris Donnelly, interview, April 1994.

12. Ibid.

13. Mary Daly, *Beyond God the Father: Toward a Philosophy of Women's Liberation* (Boston: Beacon Press, 1973), 5–8.

14. Elizabeth Johnson, CSJ, interview, April 1994.

15. Mary Luke Tobin, interview, February 1994.

16. Paulo Freire, *Pedagogy of the Oppressed* (New York: Seabury Press, 1974), 21.

17. Gerda Lerner, *The Creation of a Feminist Consciousness* (New York: Oxford University Press, 1993), 274.

18. Elizabeth Schüssler Fiorenza, *Discipleship of Equals* (New York: Crossroads, 1993), 331.

Chapter 5

PRIVILEGED AND PEDESTALED

My nightmare is that Rome wakes up and ordains some conservative vowed nuns in habits who would plug into the existing system of clericalism and take the vow of obedience to the pope.[1]

If, as was noted in chapter 2, some women in the church really do fear sisters, their anxiety presumably flows from the church's age-old practice of pitting one group against the other. So the time for women to examine the cause of that fear is long overdue. In chapter 1 attention was given to the conditioning of women in the church and how they have internalized the message of patriarchy. Only passing reference was made to the fact that sisters have also been included among those women. What was not said was that in addition to being exposed to patriarchy prior to Vatican II, sisters had received an additional formation that was not only patriarchal but militaristic as well.

Rules and constitutions for sisters were written mainly by men out of a male, militaristic model that has served men well. This training was designed to curtail affections and emotions. Uniformity was idealized; individual gifts were not recognized. A quotation from one community illustrates this militaristic model:

The beauty of an army is the perfect uniformity of every soldier in dress, in arms, in movements, etc. So likewise, every religious should be recognized at once, and everywhere, as a member of her Order.[2]

Sisters were taught to think of themselves as religious, but not necessarily as women. The clothing they wore (scapulars and capes) was designed to disguise their bodies, rendering them genderless. They wore men's shoes, carried men's umbrellas, used men's handerkerchiefs, and wore men's underwear. They were without a personal identity, given a new name, many of which were male, and not allowed to use their family name. They were oriented to dying to the

41

world, to their families, and to any type of self-identity. They underwent, in today's parlance, a brainwashing analogous to what we criticize the Moonies and other sects for doing to youth today. All this was accepted as part of the formation of a religious.

Many sisters left religious life, while the rest either ignored or endured the indoctrination. Everyone, knowingly or not, suffered some effects of this deformation. It twisted relationships between and among sisters and the laity; it warped the sisters' image of authority; it confused their sense of who they were as women and caused many to disengage from their feelings and emotions. Even today, there are some sisters who will not or cannot form healthy relationships with other women. Anger, confusion, and a low self-image were both temporary and permanent by-products of this deformation.

Sisters were told to conform, not to think, and certainly not to think critically. The development of a healthy conscience was difficult under such circumstances. Those who were creative or different were often persecuted, punished, and marginalized. In many communities, if a candidate had a college degree when she entered, she was given the lowliest tasks to make her humble. Holiness was very much related to a lockstep model of piety. Everyone was taught the same method of prayer and lived according to a regimented routine.

Added to this was the teaching of the church that the religious vocation was a step above that of the married life and/or the single life. (This is the pedestal referred to in the title of this chapter.) The "good sister" was the one who kept the rule of both the congregation and the church. She observed the rules of the cloister and did not socialize with other women. This separateness created a sense of mystery around the convent and those who lived in it. The laity did not quite know how to relate to sisters, and vice versa. It also promoted a sense of elitism on the part of sisters, and for other women, a feeling of being inferior as women in the church.

Sisters were elevated and put on a pedestal. This did little for the self-image of other women and was detrimental to all. The church canonizes women who are virgins or martyrs, but rarely married women. This certainly implies that marriage is not as holy a state as the religious life and that married women are less worthy than virgins or martyrs. Unfortunately, the exceptions are those who are young widows or women who remain faithful to husbands who abuse them both physically and psychologically, or those who die in childbirth rather than have an abortion. In 1994, Pope John Paul II beatified two women, a Zairean and an Italian, who, he said, were examples of fidelity and care for others:

Dr. Gianna Beretta Molla of Zaire, a pediatrician, was pregnant when a uterine tumor was discovered. Instead of undergoing a lifesaving operation that would have led to the death of the fetus, Molla carried the baby to term. She died at age 39 a week after the infant's birth in 1962.

Elisabetta Canori Mora, born in Rome in 1774, was beatified as an example of a Christian mother who cared for her children and helped the poor despite the hardships she faced after her husband abandoned the family. . . . The Vatican praised her fidelity to her marriage vows despite the physical and psychological abuse to which her husband subjected her.[3]

The issue is not whether these two women were worthy of beatification, but that the examples seem to indicate unless a woman chooses virginity, martyrdom, or self-immolation, the chances for sainthood are slim indeed. Women could not be given a clearer message.

Excluding those sisters who stood up to abusive pastors and bishops, the "good sisters" taught their students how to become "good women," who always defer to their husbands and to priests, never question authority, never rock the boat. In other words, they taught that women should stay in their place in society and in the church. Many women learned their lessons well and today criticize other women for not staying in their place. These women believe that being a lector, a eucharistic minister, a deacon, or, heaven forbid, a priest is not a proper role for women.

The "good sisters" also taught women to consider it a privilege to be able to clean the church, fix the flowers, and prepare everything for the priests. Those sisters knew women were not worthy to be in the sanctuary except to clean it. They were to stay home, rear children, obey their husbands, and be good wives. In fact, women were taught by the sisters that they were second-class members of the church. *The term may never have been voiced but the message was clear.* This deformation of sisters, which was built on the patriarchal conditioning of all women, made it a holy thing for them to pass on to Catholic girls and women and was extremely successful. This scenario was very familiar to those who were adults in the church before Vatican II, and to their mothers and grandmothers as well. Fortunately, there were some who did not take this formation seriously and others who quickly became aware of its crippling effects. The fact that most feminist theologians today, including sisters, are products of Catholic school education indicates that all women did not internalize this message.

In the mid-1960s and throughout the 1970s, during the so-called renewal period, many sisters left religious life. Those who stayed struggled for or against renewal in its various forms. Religious formation began to change with the advent of Vatican II and its document on the Church in the Modern World. For the most part, women who grew up in this era did not go to Catholic schools and were not the object of the "sister says" mentality. Or, if they did, their religious training was very sporadic and ill-defined because theology was in the process of changing and no one knew quite what to teach. The result is a whole generation of women and men who, on the one hand, know very little about what was taught in the Baltimore Catechism, and on the other hand, have very little patience today with a church that is trying to return to the old order. These same women are products of their culture; many work outside the home, are independent, and view marriage as a partnership and themselves as equal human beings. Consequently, for many, the church has become irrelevant. On the other hand, there are those women who want the church to be what it was before Vatican II—a safe haven where right and wrong were clearly defined—and they oppose those who speak for renewal and an egalitarian church.

What happened to the sisters? The documents of Vatican II made it clear to sisters that they were members of the laity and their vocation was not above that of married or single women. This was a shock to some and a delight to many others. Most sisters took off the habit that had kept them a neuter gender and struggled to find the women underneath. (I call this period our "just off the boat" look.) They had to learn to dress, to style their hair, to look like other women. In so doing, they lost their privileged position, which was difficult for many to accept.

In the struggle to create new forms of community, sisters experienced and continue to experience, sometimes even more than before, a great deal of oppression from one another. They encounter the silent treatment, those who refuse to confront, subtle put-downs, and petty jealousies. Sisters sometimes oppress themselves by electing leaders who either refuse, or are afraid to challenge the members of the community to be their best.

Among those who have authority, whether at the local, provincial, or higher level, there are still those who use their authority as power-over rather than power-with. They understand well the use and misuse of power. Choosing not to address issues is oppressive; not recognizing and affirming gifts in others is oppressive; overlooking the simple and ordinary sisters among them is oppressive; the use of secrecy, "I know something you don't know," is oppressive; treating the elderly like children is oppressive.

A very good question for sisters in leadership positions to reflect on is, "why did my community elect me?" Likewise, for the membership the question is, "why did I vote for this person?" The answer to the first question is integral to management style and how power is used or abused. The answer to the second question is a reflection of how each individual sister values being challenged in her religious life today. These questions are posed to raise awareness to the damage sisters can do to themselves and to others if they do not examine their ways of relating to one another.

The intellectual and emotional struggle to shed the shackles of pre-Vatican II formation was extremely difficult. In fact remnants of that formation remain in many sisters. This is seen in

— those who have removed the habit but continue to expect preferential treatment;
— those who verbalize acceptance of their lay status but continue to consider themselves superior to other women;
— those who continue to maintain a poor self-image out of a false sense of humility;
— those who accept positions in sponsored institutions without adequate qualifications;
— those who profess that they are for women but refuse to use inclusive language when they pray, or who make excuses for the priest's sexist language either because they are afraid to challenge him or they accept their second class status in the church.

There are some women who entered religious orders after Vatican II yet have still been tainted by the "privileged and pedestaled" mentality. They either have absorbed it from others, or are convinced they merit privilege. Some may even have entered in order to become privileged, whether knowingly or not.

In the mid-1960s Vatican II encouraged the laity to take their rightful place in the church. No one realized, least of all the sisters, what an effect this would have on them. The bishops certainly did not foresee how many women would take this seriously and begin studying for degrees in theology and Scripture. The growth of an educated laity competing for positions previously held by sisters had two very diverse effects: on the one hand it led to a sense of insecurity, jealousy, and distrust on the part of those sisters who viewed these educated women as invading their turf and as rivals for their jobs. On the other hand, it paved the way for the strong Catholic feminist movement uniting sisters and other women that is alive and well in today's church.

When Vatican II removed sisters from their pedestals and invited the laity to assume their rightful place in the church, it unknowingly provided the means by which women could begin to heal the divisions that patriarchy had fostered among them for centuries.

Perhaps the best story describing patriarchy's effort to divide and separate women, and the strength of sisterhood to overcome those efforts, is the story of Lilith.

According to rabbinic legend, in the beginning the Lord God formed Adam and Lilith from the dust of the ground and breathed into their nostrils the breath of life. They were equal in all ways. Adam, being a man, didn't like this situation and he looked for ways to change it. He ordered her to wait on him and tried to leave to her the daily tasks of the garden. But Lilith wasn't one to take such nonsense so she picked herself up, and flew away. Well now, Lord, said Adam, that uppity woman you sent me has gone and deserted me. The Lord, inclined to be sympathetic, sent his messengers after Lilith, telling her to shape up and return to Adam or face dire punishment. She, however, preferring anything to living with Adam, decided to stay where she was. And so God, after more careful consideration, caused a deep sleep to fall over Adam and out of one of his ribs created for Adam a second companion, Eve.

For a time everything went well with Adam and Eve. But at times Eve sensed within herself capacities that remained undeveloped. And she was lonely because God and Adam seemed to have more in common, both being men. Meanwhile Lilith, all alone, attempted at times to rejoin the human community in the garden. But Adam built the walls higher and stronger and told Eve fearsome stories of the demon Lilith who threatens women in childbirth, steals children from their cradles in the middle of the night. The second time Lilith came she stormed the gate and a great battle ensued between her and Adam in which she was finally defeated. This time, Eve got a glimpse of her and saw she was a woman like herself.

Seeds of curiosity and doubt began to grow in Eve's mind. Was Lilith just another women even though Adam had said she was a demon? How nice it would be if she were another woman. One day Eve wandered to the edge of the garden and noticed an apple tree branch that hung over the garden wall. She climbed up and swung herself over. There was Lilith waiting for her. At first Eve was afraid but Lilith greeted her kindly. "Who are you?" they asked each other. "What is your story?' They talked for many hours of the past and of the future, they laughed and cried together until the bond of sisterhood grew between them.

Meanwhile Adam and God talked about Eve's comings and goings and her new attitude toward him. And God and Adam were expectant and afraid the day Eve and Lilith returned to the garden, bursting with possibilities, ready to rebuild it together.[4]

It is clear from this story that the church, represented by Adam, has for centuries worked to keep women apart. And like Eve, women have listened to the church for all those hundreds of years. They have also realized their aloneness, but it is only since Vatican II that their awareness has slowly grown and sisters and other women have been jumping over the wall and are gradually finding out that they are very much alike. Many see that they can share their stories, talk about their past, and look to the future together. As their bonding grows stronger and their plans to rebuild the church together begin to crystalize, the patriarchal church, in the persons of the pope, the bishops, and many of the clergy, becomes more fearful of losing its power and prestige.

The story of Lilith and Eve can only be a "happily ever after" story if sisters and other women are committed to breaching the walls of suspicion, separateness, jealousy, and insecurity, and make greater efforts to raise each other up. That does not mean that they have to agree with everything other women say and do. That is an impossible expectation. Women should, as Susan Muto has put it, "at least agree to disagree agreeably." [5] Right now they are far from doing even that.

Women cannot even agree on how to refer to sisters. Many women resent sisters calling themselves "women religious" or "religious women" because many women are also religious. Sisters who cling to the title "sister" are criticized for wanting special deference, and when they drop the title are censured for not saying who they are. Elizabeth Schüssler Fiorenza uses the terms "laywomen and nun-women" in order to characterize both groups within ecclesiastical categories. She does this to call attention to alienating labels.[6] There are not many sisters who find this an acceptable solution. Could it be that the focus is misdirected and titles are not the real issue? Rather, is it not the internal baggage women carry that causes the titles to be disturbing? Perhaps it is past associations with these titles that are the source of the problem.

Over the past thirty years the struggle to overcome the divisiveness and separateness among sisters and other women has continued. When Theresa Kane, RSM, offered her famous greeting to John Paul II in 1979, she was very conscious of the deep divisions between sisters and other women, so after she greeted the pope and spoke about the work of sisters, she consciously shifted her focus and said,

> I urge you to be mindful of the intense suffering and pain which is part of the life of many women in these United States. I call upon you to listen with compassion and to hear the call of women who comprise half of humankind. As women we have heard the powerful messages of our Church addressing the dignity and reverence for all persons. As women we have pondered upon

these words. Our contemplation leads us to state that the Church in its struggle to be faithful to its call for reverence and dignity for all persons must respond by providing the possibility of women as persons being included in all ministries of our church. I urge you to be open to and respond to the voices coming from the women of this country who are desirous of serving in and through the Church as fully participating members.[7]

In her interview, Kane indicated that she did not want to give the pope a message that would have been divisive for women. Afterward, she said, a lot of Catholic women thanked her for her inclusivity.

Sister Mary Luke Tobin, SL, one of the few women auditors present at Vatican II, sensitive to the separation that existed between sisters and other women, noted, "we went through a lot of changes after Vatican II and most of us approved of those changes. We liked them." Then she pointed out what those changes were really doing was making sisters equal to other women. "The equality of all people is what we are promoting as Christians." However, many sisters see their star going down and the star of other women rising and they resent it. We are really not talking about anyone being on top but about equality, sharing, and mutuality. "Sisters," she said, "have to figure out if they are contributing to inequality in the church." If they insist on privilege, whether it is for jobs, perks, special places, or whatever, they are contributing to inequality. "We haven't gone far enough as sisters to see wherein we still accept privilege. That's something we have to work on," Tobin said.[8]

With the recognition that all women are laywomen, some sisters feel a loss of privilege and the absence of being somehow exalted or pedestaled. They envision themselves as quasi clergy and want to enjoy the benefit of a few perks. If sisters become like everybody else, they will lose those privileges. "I've made this wonderful sacrifice of my life," they might think. If they reflected even for a moment on the sacrifices married or single women with children have made, they might think twice before extolling the sacrifices of religious life.

Even today, a significant number of sisters still consider themselves privileged. A woman in the Midwest, who had attended a conference for parish ministers, related her experience with a group of sisters. They were sharing who they were and where they were from when one turned and asked her to which community she belonged. She replied that she was a director of religious education (DRE) and belonged to a parish. The sister responded, "Oh, you're an OLP." The woman didn't understand the acronym and later found that it meant, "only a lay person." The intent was to distinguish the privileged from the nonprivileged.

It should be noted that other women make this distinction also. Some women are intimidated the more sisters become like them. They want to keep sisters in their stereotyped role and image. Strong liberated sisters often pose a threat. Many would like sisters to return to wearing the habit. Others like to cater to sisters and keep them on a pedestal, where they can be watched more closely and are less threatening.

The fault does not lie solely with the sisters. Women very often defer to sisters, either individually or as a community, the rights and responsibilities that they have been taught not to claim. "Let sister run the meeting and say the prayer." Or, "Sister took a course on that, let her tell us what to do." Women defer too much to sisters, even when they themselves know the topic as well or better and, unfortunately, some sisters allow this to continue. Prior to Vatican II, the exaltation of religious life was part of the teaching of the church, which was reinforced by the sisters. Even today, some sisters still promote this teaching and expect such deference. Neither behavior contributes to the leveling of differences so needed before women can relate to one another as equals.

In cases where sisters and other women compete for the same positions or for ministries traditionally reserved to members of religious orders, some sisters assume that, regardless of qualifications, they should have job preference.

Even today, sisters are placed in positions of authority without always being adequately prepared. They face well-trained women and feel threatened. Some are willing to work for less pay in order to obtain or keep a position. The expectations of sisters and other women of one another are often distorted and confused. Sisters accuse other women of taking their jobs and vice versa simply because the two rarely sit down and talk. The woman might think the sister really does not need the job because she has the security of community backing, not knowing the sister is responsible to her community for generating a certain income to support herself and the elderly. Conversely, the sister might surmise the woman's husband has a good job, but have no idea of the woman's needs. Shared dialogue could turn their oppressive behavior into understanding, mutuality, and support. As long as women continue to refer to one another as "them" and "us" they will never accept each other as equals and be able to work together toward an egalitarian church.

Any oppressed group has its place within the structure; women in the church are no exception. They are used, given minor ministries (i.e., as altar servers but not as deaconesses); they have an identity even if it is second class; they know their place. Some women are reluctant to move out of that place and be treated as equals because they fear all will be lost. This phenomenon is described by Paulo Freire as "the fear of freedom."

> The "fear of freedom" which afflicts the oppressed is one of the basic elements of the relationship between oppressor and oppressed. . . . Thus, the behavior of the oppressed is a prescribed behavior, following as it does the guidelines of the oppressor. The oppressed, having internalized the image of the oppressor and adopted his guidelines, are fearful of freedom. Freedom would require them to eject this image and replace it with autonomy and responsibility.[9]

When women move out of their traditional place, they have no place, are not welcomed by the clergy, and are ostracized and marginalized by other women. Because they must endure that period of limbo, there is continued resistance on the part of women to break out of the mold.

Sandra Schneiders tells us that is what has happened with sisters. As long as they were "good sisters" they had a certain authority, position, and even some clout in the church with special perks and privileges. They were, in her terms, "kept women," and, they were kept rather well. However, when they ceased being "good sisters," took off the veil, and began speaking out, they were no longer regarded as "good sisters," and they lost their privileged status. Sisters went through an in-between period when they had to find a whole new way of doing things, finding their own jobs, and financing their own retirement.[10]

Some sisters work in parishes and are successful in undermining the patriarchal system. They try to accomplish what would not be done in their absence. Others are still father's little helpers, embracing the system in order to retain their benefits or because their theology and spirituality are in accord with the pastor's. Since parish women frequently view sisters as "pseudo-Marys," their behavior can influence women either to remain submissive, second-class members of the church or to stand against the tide of clerical oppression by speaking and acting for justice and women's equality. Their responsibility is a grave one and sisters need to continually challenge themselves with such questions as:

— What privileges do I still hang on to that separate me from other women? Can I let go of them?
— What is it that precludes my ability to enjoy another woman's success and lift her up?
— What makes me want to sabotage other women's endeavors or success?
— When I have a position of power and authority why do I find it so difficult to reach out and raise up other women?

Sister Mary Luke Tobin puts all of these questions in perspective when she says:

Many young women are dreaming of a day when equality will be realized in the church. Sisters in American communities have come a long way. Accepting the change in the habit was a huge step forward. It was a way of coming to this whole reality of our equality; of bringing other women into our midst; of ceasing to consider it a privileged place apart where we can be separate and somehow holier. We must realize the holiness of every person and their willingness to grow in it. We have a long way to go.[11]

The bent over woman in the gospel, who for eighteen years could only see her own feet, is a symbol of women's experience in the church. Jesus came and cured her so that she could stand straight and she immediately began to praise God. When Jesus raised her up he raised up all women but throughout the centuries, the patriarchal church has steadfastly kept women bent over. Both sisters and other women have been so deformed that they could not see each other's pain. All they could see was their own feet.

As far back as the 1830s, Sarah Grimke, one of the first feminists of the last century, stated, "I ask no favors for my sex . . . all I ask our brethren is that they will take their feet from off our necks and permit us to stand upright on that ground which God designed us to occupy." [12]

Women today must join forces to remove those feet, in order to stand straight, look each other in the eye, and join hands for the equality of all.

Joan Chittister pointed out that initially sisters responded to the women's agenda far ahead of other women, but to date, in many ways, they have done less in society than other women. In the 1960s sisters raised questions in a systematic way through such organizations as the Leadership Conference of Women Religious. They began to challenge exclusive language and some liturgical practices. Women's groups had access to more resources, however, and focused on single-issue questions such as women's ordination. Since they were outside the structure of the institutional church they had a freedom to do things that sisters could not do. Women did not get permission, they just did it! Many sisters struggled to effect change within the structure with much less freedom. Others, frustrated with these limitations, formed support groups such as the National Assembly of Women Religious (NAWR) and Network, to work more freely for renewal.

In the last ten years, Chittister noted, women have gone leaping ahead into courts, into businesses, into economic independence. They are making the structural changes that many sisters realized theoretically years before. "I don't like to pit sisters and other women against each other," she said. "I see the bonding that's going on between them as one of the most beautiful and one of the most dangerous signs in the church today."[13] Could this be what John

XXIII referred to when he noted the rising consciousness of women as one of the signs of our times? We read in Matthew's gospel, 16:2–4, when the Pharisees and Sadducees asked Jesus to show them a sign, he gave this reply:

> In the evening you say, "Red sky at night the day will be bright"; but in the morning, "sky red and gloomy, the day will be stormy." If you know how to interpret the look of the sky, can you not read the signs of the times?

Vatican II made giant strides in reading the signs of the times. It not only called the church to be alert to those signs but also to be more attentive to the message of Jesus. Because of that call Catholic women, like Lilith and Eve, must struggle to strengthen the bond of sisterhood and eagerly rebuild the church together.

NOTES

1. Miriam Therese Winter, Adair Lummis, and Allison Stokes, *Defecting in Place* (New York: Crossroad, 1994), 75.
2. Rules of the Congregation of the Sisters of the Holy Cross, 1933–65, Rule 34, "Spirit of Union and Community," 231.
3. "John Paul Beatifies Zairean, Italian Women," *National Catholic Reporter,* 30, no. 27, (6 May 1994): 10.
4. Carol P. Christ and Judith Plaskow, eds., *Womanspirit Rising: A Feminist Reader in Religion* (San Francisco: Harper & Row, 1979), 206–7.
5. Susan Muto, interview, April 1994.
6. Elizabeth Schüssler Fiorenza, *Discipleship of Equals: A Critical Feminist Ekklesia-logy of Liberation* (New York: Crossroad, 1993), 183n. 2.
7. Teresa Kane, RSM, "Papal Greeting," in the Shrine of the Immaculate Conception, Washington, D. C. (October 1979).
8. Mary Luke Tobin, interview, February 1994.
9. Paulo Freire, *Pedagogy of the Oppressed* (New York: Continuum, 1993), 28–29.
10. Sandra Schneider, interview, April 1994.
11. Tobin, interview, February 1994.
12. Gerda Lerner, *The Grimke Sisters from South Carolina; Rebels Against Slavery* (Boston: Houghton Mifflin, 1967), 192.
13. Joan Chittister, interview, April 1994.

Chapter 6

Injustice Burns the Soul

I fear the struggle for justice for women in the church will be a long one. However, to be silent, or worse, to be indifferent when facing injustice is sinful.[1]

The injustice that burns the souls of conscientious Catholics today is the institutional church's blindness to the fact that in elevating and glorifying men they minimalize, marginalize, and devalue women. Because of the size, power, and visibility of the Roman Catholic Church the world over, the effects of its attitude toward women are far-reaching. The church sends a clear message that it is not just all right to negate and ignore the gifts of half of the human race, but that this has been and is God's will for women.

Time, in turn, honored the pope as "Man of the Year" in 1994, the very year that he published a gender-exclusive translation of *The Catechism of the Catholic Church* and a strong papal letter rejecting not only the possibility of women's ordination but even the right to discuss it, and supported the rejection of moderately inclusive English-language translations of the Bible for liturgical and catechetical use. As Richard McBrien observed,

> If someone in the Vatican had, on New Year's Day, 1994, secretly forged a plan to alienate as many Catholic women as possible during 1994 . . . how would that plan have differed from the actual sequence of events? Surely, no one in the Vatican set out to do this on purpose. But should that make us all feel better about what actually happened?[2]

As *Time* newsmaker of the year, what John Paul II represents is reverenced and idolized by many Catholics and non-Catholics alike. Thus, the message that women are less equal than men is reinforced.

History is replete with examples of inequality, prejudice, injuries to, and discrimination against women. As long as the church continues to function within a patriarchal infrastructure that devalues women, they will remain marginalized. The tragedy is that these outrages have not adequately stirred peoples' consciences nor roused a sufficient number of women and men to stand together against them. There are still too many "good women" in the church. Their souls do not burn with a holy anger at the injustices the church continues to perpetuate against them. However, what does burn the souls of some is that the majority of churchgoing women still use as a holy guide what the hierarchy tells them constitutes a "good woman." This affirmation empowers the clergy to keep women in a subservient position. If these women's souls do not burn at this injustice, it behooves them to examine closely what it is the clergy teaches them to be and do in order to become "good women."

According to traditional church teaching, a "good woman" accepts without question her assigned secondary place; she obeys all church teachings without protest; she defers to the priest, the bishop, and the pope in all matters of judgment; she does not think of questioning the hierarchy's definition of "separate but equal" ministries for men and women; she never ruffles the waters nor does she ever stand against the tide of clerical oppression. In other words, she agrees to have her entire persona defined by the male clergy—to her own detriment. What burns the souls of many women is that these "good women" allow men to limit and define their role. Thus all women are deprived of benefitting from the wisdom and insight of the women who exemplify most clearly women's true identity in the church.

> What we know about Christian women, their activities and ideas, until recently, is the product of patriarchal censorship. Women's ideas were censored, both in their lifetimes and after their deaths, to make them conform to male theological and social definitions of good women. And women themselves, in order to win approval and avoid punishment, conformed their own lives and ideas to this standard.[3]

How many of these women have ever wondered how Jesus might define a "good woman" today? Could they, even for a moment, imagine that Jesus' definition would bear any resemblance to what they have internalized from centuries of patriarchal teaching? Would Jesus have ever told women they were second-class? Rather, did he not include among his followers even women who, like the one who anointed his feet, were a bother or an embarrassment to his disciples? Did he ever tell women to accept his word without questioning? His discussions with the Samaritan and Canaanite women speak to the contrary. Did Jesus ever marginalize women and forbid them to dialogue with him about their status? Then why should the patriarchal church? Did Jesus ever refer to anything he taught as a message for men only or for men first? On the contrary, Jesus made it very clear who his disciples were, "Whoever does the will of God is my mother, my sister and my brother."[4]

Jesus is the model for all Christians. Yet, he did not conform to the image of the Messiah that lived in the hearts and minds of his apostles or the scribes and pharisees. He stood against the tide of religious and social injustice and was crucified for it. He said to his disciples and to all of us, "If any of you want to come after me, you must deny yourselves and take up your cross and follow me."[5] Women who want to follow Jesus now understand that following means thinking for themselves, questioning patriarchal prejudice, and standing against unjust treatment of women in the church.

Women in society, in the professions, and, lamentably, in the church are faced with injustice, inequity, and prejudice as a matter of course in their daily lives. Some few struggle against it continuously because it truly does burn their souls to be victims of bigotry and insult simply because of their gender. Many others may protest at times, because they feel scorched or singed, but are not burned deeply enough and soon retreat from the struggle, often making excuses for "the system." This behavior was epitomized by a sister who, professing to support women's equality, agreed to give a reflection after Communion rather than a homily at the liturgy when the bishop presided. In his absence she consistently preached the homily, but refused to disagree with him for fear that he could or would stop the practice altogether. This sister is a symbol for many. The question seems to be, when is discretion the better part of valor?

Still other women, in even greater numbers, may feel a sear now and then but remain indifferent and unconcerned, choosing to ignore the affronts, not willing to "get involved." They are aware, but feel it is not their responsibility, nor do they want to invest their energy trying to change things. These women keep silent and by doing so, contribute to ongoing offenses against themselves and other women.

> The greatest damage I have done to other women is probably by my modelling of acquiescence to various church institutional structures, reinforcing and promoting in a highly visible and even at times, attractive way, the delicate art of being a clerical 'helpmate,' accepting my role of second-class citizenship in the church and fearing to rock the boat.[6]

Lastly, there are those women who accept injustices as women's lot in life. They compound and complicate the injury to all women by their passive acceptance of a male-dominated society and church.

I was once a part of the Catholic Charismatic movement in the church. Even though this movement has many women leaders, I don't remember a single time in which they spoke out against the oppressiveness of the church's patriarchal behavior. [Married Woman, Virginia]

Women in my parish tell me there's nothing wrong, you just want power. You're not really Catholic if you don't obey the priest. [Married Woman, New York]

I find women friends become silent and very uncomfortable when I press for change or confront priests. [Single Woman, Ohio]

A prime example of indifference in the face of injustice is that of a sister in California who admitted she counseled the women in her parish to "be patient, just wait, things will change," knowing all along she did not really believe it herself, and because she was not making waves, things would never change.

Women who burn with indignation and anger because of the church's sins of injustice have entered into the painful battle for equality. They are fighting a monumental campaign, not only against the clergy and multitudes of defensive males, but also against other women. Dialogue is crucial to changing behavior, but as soon as a labeled "feminist" speaks, she often becomes marginalized by other women. Discussion is ended, the subject is changed, and she is prevented from sharing the passion aroused by the injustice that burns her soul. Some women do not want to hear it, let alone discuss it, while others cannot risk the chance that there might be a fire smoldering within them. Still others turn away either because they have been conditioned to accept their status as the norm or because they are indifferent, lukewarm, or afraid to be marginalized themselves.

However, there are women who, regardless of the consequences, move to action when their souls burn. A case in point is that of a sister who participated in the liturgy at a male-dominated university. After listening to a homily that avoided any mention of the bent over woman in the gospel reading for that day, she marched into the sacristy and confronted the priest. "Look out there and tell me who the majority of the congregation are," she said. When he acknowledged that they were women, she went on, "We women hear so little about our gender in this church. When you have the opportunity to preach to women about women, please do! Our souls hunger for some recognition of the fact that we also belong to this church." Apparently, she was the only woman who was moved to action by the fire for justice burning in her soul. What of the others? Were they indifferent, lukewarm, satisfied with what they heard, or just too timid to object? Was there even a spark of indignation among them?

56

Is it possible to ignite a fire for justice in women who seemingly do not have even a spark? Jesus came to light a fire on the earth and expressed great desire that it be ignited. Women who continually work to keep the fire of indignation suppressed are refusing to allow the spark of the Spirit they received in baptism to grow into a fire for justice. If they persist in permitting the patriarchal church to asphyxiate them as it has suffocated women for centuries, what will happen to women's struggle for justice in the church? The seriousness of this dilemma is highlighted by a Catholic feminist when speaking of women's efforts to redeem humanity from patriarchy,

> The outcome of this conflict is unclear, but what is indisputable is that Christianity, for the first time in its history, is faced with a large-scale challenge to the patriarchal interpretation of religion and an increasingly coherent vision of an alternative way of constructing the tradition from its very roots. The question for the future is perhaps not so much whether this alternative will prevail, as whether it will survive and continue to be a public option for the next generation of Christians, or whether its very existence will again be erased from the public memory of the churches, only to have to be reinvented and rediscovered again by a future generation of women.[7]

We cannot deny the entanglement of women in patriarchal behavior, but we can plead for women's conversion. Elizabeth Schüssler Fiorenza warns women about the deadly dangers and failures that threaten feminist movements in the church today. Such failures include:

— psychologism, which does not allow for any critical debate, but infantilizes women by "mothering" them;
— anti-intellectualism, which understands serious intellectual work as male and therefore unfeminine;
— horizontal violence, which thrashes strong women who refuse to remain feminine victims;
— guilt-tripping and confessionalism, which repeat the litany of patriarchy's sins without ever doing anything about them;
— exclusivism, which insists on women-church as the gathering of the truly true feminists and which dehumanizes men as evil.[8]

In the face of these dangers, she reminds women that they need a spirituality that understands fear, co-optation, betrayal, and feminist burnout and that they must:

Keep alive the burning indignation at the destructive powers of patriarchy in women's lives—an indignation that fuels the courage and faith necessary in the struggle for survival and liberation. Only if we keep this holy anger alive will we sustain the courage and love that is necessary to work for the conversion and transformation of the patriarchal church into the discipleship of equals.[9]

"Until there is anger," argued a woman from Louisiana, "justice will not be done!" "But, in order to have that anger," another woman responded, "you have to have some conscious experience of injustice." You have to believe that you are worth being treated justly.

Too many women in society as well as in the church are victims of their own poor self-image and, consequently, it is impossible for them to feel a burning indignation in the face of patriarchal injustices.

How can you burn with anger against injustice if you don't feel it? Unfortunately, too many women are unaware that they are discriminated against, as is evidenced by the totality of their conditioning by the patriarchal church.

Even in language some women insist the term "men" includes both sexes. They believe that the status quo is permanently ordained by God. They dismiss my beliefs and actions as wrong or silly, using the power system to prevent things from happening. [Sister, Colorado]

I feel that women who think the organization of the church is divinely ordained, that it came directly from God, are an obstacle to those of us working for equality of women and men in the church. [Married Woman, Indiana]

Women who are most oppressive to other women are very often insecure in themselves. A woman from the south indicated, "I don't feel good enough to minister in the church so why should I support other women in ministry?"

A powerful example of such behavior was related by theologian Dody Donnelly from her own class in masculine spirituality. The students were mostly women. She invited a panel composed of a psychologist, a sociologist, a theologian, and an anthropologist, all top men in their fields, to make a presentation to the class. The excitement was intense as the women interviewed the presenters, even continuing beyond class time. The men left feeling validated and affirmed. Two weeks later, she invited a panel of top women, some even more noted in their fields. The difference in the response of the students was indicative of the effects of patriarchal conditioning on women. There was no excitement, there were very few questions, and there was little interest shown in the accomplishments of these outstanding women. The panel left without receiving either validation or affirmation. Donnelly noted that this was especially painful because the students saw nothing wrong with their conduct. On the contrary, the class protested that they were for women!

Donnelly's assessment of the class' behavior was posed as both a question and an answer: "Why don't women prize other women's gifts? Because," she maintains, "they have never had their own prized. When women deny their own and other's gifts, they are simply repeating the sins of patriarchy."[10]

Women are taught to value themselves from their culture, their education, their parents, and so on. Yet young women go through a deselfing period beginning in high school when they internalize messages indicating they are not supposed to be as smart as the boys, that there are few rewards for being smart, and that often there are punishments. The message is not as blatant as it once was, but it still exists today. Young women often gain approval from their parents if they are beautiful, attractive to the opposite sex, gain admittance to a good sorority, and ultimately marry well. There is a direct relationship between how young women value themselves and are valued by others and how sucessfully they fulfill these expectations.

In her work in spiritual direction, Dody Donnelly meets with many women who are trying to reclaim their selfhood either from a bad marriage experience or from being "de-selfed" in a university, business, or church-related experience. In other words, she explains, "women are throw-away material. I think this is probably the sickness of this century that their gifts are not being used by half the human race."[11]

The church tells women that ordination is not a matter of justice because no one has a right to be ordained; rather, it is a gift from God given only to men. The pope tells women that their gender is the only barrier to ordination and hence to full participation in church ministry. While claiming to be a just institution, the church continues to reserve all decision making to a few celibate males, while women continue to comprise the majority of churchgoers and parish ministers. If an unjust law is that which demeans human beings, we must ask ourselves what could be more demeaning to women than John Paul II's "definitive statement" prohibiting even the discussion of women's ordination? Women are faced with one of two conclusions: either the pope's statement is unjust or he does not consider women fully human. Although we now have a growing collection of church documents affirming the dignity, equality, and giftedness of women, these documents offer no greater clarity or specificity about what steps the church intends to take to offer women roles affirming that equality. This injustice continues to burn the souls of Catholic feminists.

The sins of patriarchy are certainly grave, but women who sin by indifference, silence, lukewarmness and overt oppression of other women in the face of the church's injustice against them are equally sinful. Until more women begin to nurture the fire for justice they received at Baptism and cease allowing the patriarchal church to smother the spark of the Spirit within them, women's struggle for justice in the church will be prolonged.

Notes

1. Miriam Therese Winter, Adair Lummis, and Allison Stokes, *Defecting in Place* (New York: Crossroad, 1994), 87.
2. Richard P. McBrien, "Confusing the Laity" in *Fellowship of Southern Illinois Laity* (Belleville, Ill.: 28 November 1994).
3. Rosemary Radford Ruether, "Sexism as Ideology and Social System: Can Christianity Be Liberated from Patriarchy?," in *With Both Eyes Open,* Patricia Altenbernd Johnson and Janet Kalven, eds., (New York: Pilgrim Press, 1988), 153.
4. *The New Testament of the Inclusive Language Bible* (Notre Dame, Ind.: Cross Cultural Publications, Cross Roads Books, 1994), Mk 3:35.
5. Ibid., Matthew 16:24.
6. Interview, sister in California.
7. Ruether, "Sexism as Ideology," 163.
8. Elizabeth Schüssler Fiorenza, *Discipleship of Equals* (New York: Crossroad, 1993), 330–31.
9. Ibid., 331.
10. Dody Donelly, interview, February 1994.
11. Ibid.

Chapter 7

SHEDDING THE SHACKLES

What power is it that makes a Hindu woman burn herself on the funeral pyre of her husband? Her religion. What holds the Turkish woman in the harem? Her religion. By what power do Mormons perpetuate their system of polygamy? By their religion. Man, of himself, could not do this; but when he declares, 'thus says the Lord,' of course he can do it. So long as ministers [priests] stand up and tell us that as Christ is the head of the church so is man the head of the woman, how are we to break the chains which have held women down through the ages?[1]

E lizabeth Cady Stanton, a great feminist of the nineteenth century, traveled the world searching for the source of women's oppression and their subordination to men. She found it in the very institutions that give lip service to the equality of all men and women. Is it not amazing that she found the cause of women's oppression over a hundred years ago?

The Catholic Church's contribution to this oppression is exemplified in the words of St. Clement of Alexandria: "Every woman should be filled with shame by the thought that she is a woman."[2] So also in St. Augustine, who argued

> that woman together with her husband is in the image of God . . . but when she is referred to separately . . . she is not the image of God, but as regards man alone, he is the image of God as fully and completely as when the woman too is joined with him in one.[3]

In a work on the *Sacrament of Orders*, published in 1962 by Emmanuel D'Lorenzo, O.M.I., then on the theology faculty of the Catholic University of America, D'Lorenzo teaches that

> the reason . . . for denying women the right to teach is a reason that is absolute and universal, based as it is on the natural condition of inferiority and

subjection that is the portion of women. This moral feebleness is manifest at once in lightness of judgment, in credulity . . . and finally in the fragility of spirit by which she is less able to reign in the passions, particularly concupiscence.[4]

Teachings and practices of the church over the centuries have masked or even attempted to eradicate the indelible sign of baptism on the souls of women by disabling them with the shackle of unworthiness.

By their baptism Christians have been called to be Christ wherever they are. The early Christians learned this from Paul and incorporated his words into their baptismal formula: "There is neither Jew nor Gentile, slave nor free, male nor female. You are all one in Christ Jesus."[5] Two thousand years later in the *Catechism of the Catholic Church* Christians read the same message:

> Incorporated into Christ by Baptism, the person baptized is configured to Christ. Baptism seals the Christian with the indelible spiritual mark (character) of his[her] belonging to Christ. No sin can erase this mark, even if sin prevents Baptism from bearing the fruits of salvation. Given once for all, Baptism cannot be repeated.[6]

In explaining the nature of the indelible spiritual mark to children, *The Saint Joseph Baltimore Catechism* states, "A character is a mark on the soul like a seal on soft wax. It stamps the image of Christ on the soul and gives the soul a share in the priestly powers of Christ."[7]

It would seem the grace of baptism as described and taught by the church is more than sufficient for women and men alike to respond to the Holy Spirit's urging to be Christ wherever they are since both are stamped with the image of Christ.

The spirituality of women all over the world has been warped by the church's continued emphasis on their sinfulness. It began with Eve's supposed responsibility for the fall of the human race and has continued throughout history with its emphasis on women's uncleanliness and need for purification— to women as a constant source of temptation.

The fact that the Vatican insists that women cannot be priests, because it would be difficult to see how they image Christ, begs the question, whatever happened to the indelible stamp of the image of Christ on women's souls?

Throughout the ages, women have been deprived of their baptismal rights by the strength of patriarchy, and many do not fully understand the meaning of baptism either for themselves or for men. Women's deep love for the church often precludes accepting the fact that this church to which they are so committed is built on a structure that is detrimental to the spiritual health of all.

Women also receive conflicting messages from the clergy and hierarchy, from priests who do not show respect for women to a cardinal proposing women be lay cardinals; and from the pope maintaining women's exclusion from the priesthood is in accordance with God's plan for the church to the bishops' committee proclaiming with certainty that discrimination against women contradicts the will of Christ.[8]

The patriarchal shackle that attempts to efface women's baptismal character is the stamp of "unworthiness" superimposed by the clergy. The painful struggle Catholic feminists are currently engaged in is to shed this shackle and rediscover the mark of their baptism.

To be Christ requires more than words. It requires heroic action. Michael Crosby, OFM, Cap., maintains "Jesus was not killed because he preached the beatitudes to his disciples, but because he came down the mountain and put his preaching into practice, he concretized it in his behavior."[9] Women who follow the example of Jesus will not only dare to speak about codiscipleship but will be moved to heroic action. As Mary Collins has stated:

> Women who make a decision to take a clear position and to stand against patriarchal structures do the whole community a clear service. They provide other women the opportunity of finding their own place on the continuum. It also means that people can make a decision and have to sort out their motives, why they stay, what their values are. Any of us who are functioning in the Roman Catholic church are in that situation.[10]

Women who come to resolution and begin to act earn the right to advocate equality and justice because they have entered into the struggle.

Catholic women have been indoctrinated to believe that the patriarchal system is, in fact, God's will for the church. However, it is women's loyalty to the institutional church rather than loyalty to their faith that becomes oppressive.

Consider women who believe that whatever the pope says should be accepted as gospel even though their hearts and minds tell them otherwise. Or visualize the numerous convents where pictures of the pope, the bishop of the diocese, and the pastor still hold places of honor even though the sisters in those houses feel oppressed by these same clergy. This behavior is even more explicit in religious communities when a tyrannical bishop is repeatedly invited to preside at jubilee or profession ceremonies. What are the ramifications of this misplaced loyalty? Few women are consciously aware of how oppressive this behavior is to other women, and even fewer are willing or able to change.

If faith in a compassionate, inclusive Jesus who treated all people with dignity and respect is integral to our Catholic faith, why do so many women continue to give their allegiance to an oppressive, exclusive, hierarchical church?

We saw in chapter 2 how the personal needs of many women for security, affirmation, and approval seem to supersede their ability to take a stand against those responsible for injustices against women in the church. Unfortunately, so many women's unconscious co-optation into the "God's will" syndrome of patriarchy keeps them loyal to the system and unable to see its sins. They fail to understand the implications of their own behavior and would rather feed on the crumbs from the clerical table than pay the price for the bread of life promised to those who seek justice.[11] This shackle of misplaced belief causes women to act out of fear and insecurity, and often the focus of their actions is other women. Some elect to be dependent and weak, remaining as "God's little children" in a warped sense. Rosemary Radford Ruether challenges this dependency when she says:

> The key question is whether feminists in the churches will be silenced, lower their profile, feel that they can only survive by appearing more conventional. Or whether feminists will see this as the critical teaching moment, the time when it becomes essential for feminists to bond together across denominations, to organize some very well-done, clear, pastoral communication that would go out both to church leadership and to ordinary parishes? In other words, to enter the struggle for the soul of the church.[12]

If women were to rise to Ruether's challenge and bond together, they would indeed be an imposing force.

The use and misuse of power by some clergy is the principal cause of many women's fear of assuming power in the church. Their experience of being exploited and manipulated by the hierarchy, along with their knowledge of the clergy's competitive climb up the ecclesiastical ladder, convinces many that the structure must be changed. Women realize that incorporating themselves into existing structures is not the answer.

Some women operate from a sense of false humility or self-doubt, preferring to remain helpless and submissive in the face of patriarchal power. Others refuse to assume power because the price of marginalization is too high. Some resist other women's use of power because they are not willing to entrust authority to another woman. Each of these behaviors keeps women separated and at odds with each other.

As women grapple with the shackle of power in the church, they should be aware of important insights as well as significant questions they must address. First,

— power cannot be given, it must be shared, and this requires strength and purpose;

— those who have power must begin by listening to others;

— taking a stand can be a positive experience because it frequently results from the empowerment of others;

— power must be grounded in something beyond the self, i.e., justice, enablement, dialogue, equalization of power;

— there is no way to pursue justice outside the realm of love and Jesus is our model here as in all our actions;

— baptism empowers one to live the mission of Jesus.

These insights prompt the following questions:

— what will women sacrifice to realize their equality in the church?

— will women imitate the patriarchal model they have been victims of for centuries? Or,

— will women seek to create webs of shared power, including men and women alike?

The question of the use and misuse of power is complex. We need only remind ourselves that some men and women have always objected to women gaining power and authority. Since there is no other accepted model, such people fear women will start treating men the same way men have treated women. Likewise, women of this mind-set fear even more that women will start treating women the way men have treated women.

The vision of shared power or codiscipleship must occupy women's attention. For them, learning to be partners is far less threatening. It is also much more difficult to do.

> The chance that women will try to dominate men is scant. But the chance that women will get fed up with men who refuse to learn partnership is real . . . These women may simply pack up and leave.[13]

Prior to Vatican II the meaning of being "Catholic" was eminently clear to all. What Catholics could or could not do, what they must believe, and how they should pray was articulated by the clergy. The faithful internalized the message. Men knew their place in the church; women certainly knew theirs.

However, what it means to be "Catholic" at the close of the twentieth century is difficult to discern. There are no clear definitions. Even the *Catechism of the Catholic Church* contains ambiguities and ambivalences that those who composed the *Baltimore Catechism* could never have imagined.

Some women who have internalized the old formula of what it means to be Catholic find it difficult if not impossible to accept those whose definition of "Catholic" is far broader, less clerically determined, and more attractive to feminists. The former, tied to their belief and pious practices, cannot imagine another kind of church. The latter, freed from numerous old restraints, are struggling to create a new vision of church. And a third group, described as "middle-of-the-roaders," include women who have one foot in the old Catholic tradition and the other in the new. They cannot seem to move either forward or backward.

The division among these groups of women means they are controlled by patriarchy. Women on the far right are rewarded for conforming to the thinking of conservative clergy, while those on the far left are marginalized as objects of fear and suspicion. The middle-of-the-road women shuffle between the two, feeling smothered by the old ways and frightened of the new, or remain indifferent to it all.

To free themselves from a divisiveness fueled by patriarchy, misdirected mentors, and a lack of feminist visionaries, women must struggle with the questions posed by Rosemary Radford Ruether:

> Is the essential vision of this community [the church] that of patriarchal hierarchy in which women are subordinate members of the Christian community?
>
> If the Christian community isn't about being a healthy and redemptive community, then what is it about?
>
> Are the patriarchal female-scapegoating patterns of Christianity essential and irreformable, or are they a distortion that can be critiqued in the light of a more authentic vision of the Gospel?[14]

In addition to divisiveness, the deformation of women is perhaps the one shackle that has been most successful in defacing the baptismal character that configures women's souls to Christ. Whether single, married, divorced, widowed, or sisters, women suffer some damage from their Christian formation. You may be saying to yourself, "not I, I don't feel I have been damaged." If so, you are either extremely fortunate or unable to recognize your own wounds.

Many will never recover completely from the wounds the institutional church has inflicted on them. They are plagued with distorted expectations of one another, misdirected fear and anger, and an inability to claim the gifts of their baptism. Is it any wonder that so many of today's Catholic women are either unwilling or unable to extricate themselves from this shackle and are questioning why the church continues to baptize them?

Some women, graced by working with a visionary liturgist, a priest who promotes women's equality, or other women struggling to free themselves from their own deformation, are experiencing a glimpse of what it means to be included in the church. A woman from the Midwest shares her own awakening:

> A new movement that has happened to me of late comes from being in liturgies that use or do not use inclusive language. I am so inculturated that I often do not even hear when all male language is used. I listen and the words pass over me like a stream runs over well-worn stone. I don't notice the wearing down. When I hear language that includes me like 'daughters of God,' 'Women of faith,' or 'God, our Mother,' some part of me that has not been touched begins to respond and awaken. I come out of my inner world of prayer with a sense of excitement. I have been spoken to! I am being sung about! . . . I am included in this prayer in a way that feeds me, delights me and allows me to share that joy with others. [Married Woman, Indiana]

This excitement unfortunately is in jeopardy. The Vatican's reversal, in the fall of 1994, of its approval for even moderately inclusive language translations of the Bible for liturgical and catechetical use in the United States indicates its unwillingness or inability to recognize women as full members of the church. This action was exclusive, punitive, and severely detrimental to the spiritual life of the entire Catholic community, men as well as women. When women work against the use of inclusive language they deprive all women of the joy, excitement, and nourishment described above. This prolongs women's deformation, by keeping them excluded or marginalized.

According to feminist theologian Judith Plaskow, the male images of God are comforting because they are familiar. But they are also harmful because they support a religious system that has considered women to be marginally important.

> When God is pictured as male in a community that understands "man" to have been created in God's image, it only makes sense that maleness functions as the norm. . . . When maleness becomes normative, women are necessarily Other, excluded . . . and subordinated in the community . . . And when women are Other, it seems only fitting and appropriate to speak of God in language drawn from the male norm.[15]

In *A Letter to Women* in July 1995, Pope John Paul II repeatedly thanked women for their contributions to society and to the church. He stressed their importance, yet he continues to limit their mention in the liturgical language of the church. Language can build self-esteem and personal worth. When a priest speaks to the congregation as "brothers and sisters" rather than simply "brothers," women feel included. In cases where a priest continually uses sexist language, women should dare to speak up and encourage more inclusivity rather than sit silently, accepting exclusion.

Like deformation, the practice of labeling women is a shackle that pits women against women. Labels stick, and the longer they stick the more indelibly their meaning is imprinted on the mind and soul of the labeled. Some labels are applied to mislead. Others can be ignored. Yet, the more detrimental are impossible to overlook.

Definitions and labels such as "good woman/good sister," "radical feminist," or just plain "feminist" have shackled women for too long and obscured their true value. To uncover the truth or to give authentic meaning to these labels is the challenge to women everywhere.

Who, better than women, can and should define in the light of the gospel what it means to be a "good woman" or a "good sister"? We must not leave these definitions in the hands of clerics. In chapter 6 reference was made to how Jesus might have described a "good woman." His description bears no resemblance whatsoever to the depiction of the traditional church.

It is Catholic women today, who are striving to live their baptismal vows to the fullest with a radical commitment to the gospel, who will give genuine meaning to the term "good women."

Who is more qualified to explain the meaning of "feminist" or "radical feminist"? Feminist theologians have explored and explained this term in numerous ways, yet, as Sandra Schneiders observes,

> Most people understand the term "feminism" sufficiently well to react viscerally when it is used. But if asked to define the term, much less come to agreement with others about what it means or designates, they often find themselves reduced to vague generalities.[16]

Schneiders notes that there is extreme theoretical and practical diversity within the feminist movement and among feminists themselves, even though there is, as it were, a family resemblance among all feminists. Her own definition gives insight into why so many of the clergy use the term in a derogatory way:

> Feminism is a comprehensive ideology which is rooted in women's experience of sexual oppression, engages in a critique of patriarchy as an essential

dysfunctional system, embraces an alternative vision for humanity and the earth, and actively seeks to bring this vision to realization.[17]

However, too many Catholic women continue to allow the clerical innuendoes implied in comments like, "oh, you're one of those!" to overshadow and cripple them.

Who are better prepared than Catholic women to understand the ramifications of the shackles of patriarchy? Who can better understand the necessity of liberation from both clerical and female oppression? Women will not gain this liberation by chance or by waiting for the hierarchy or other women to give it to them. They will only gain it by altering their behavior: by a willingness to pay the price and by realizing the need to fight for it.

> And this fight, because of the purpose given it by the oppressed, will actually constitute an act of love opposing the lovelessness which lies at the heart of the oppressors' violence, lovelessness even when clothed in false generosity.[18]

But, as was indicated in chapter 4, some oppressed women, instead of striving for liberation, tend themselves to become oppressors. Their whole formation has conditioned and shaped their thought process. Their ideal is to be like men, their only model. As one theologian clearly observed, "When a man looks in a mirror he sees a human being. When a woman looks in a mirror she sees a woman. Malehood is the norm and is invisible."[19] The closer you are to the norm, the more invisible you become, because you are like everyone else. And who does not want to be like everyone else? It is painful to be on the margins, to be different, to speak up and out. That is why we have so many "good women" in the church.

However, there are strong women who, according to Winter, Lummis, and Stokes, are "defecting in place" in today's church. They are daring to be different; to struggle to discard the psychological chains of their deformation; and to claim the gifts of their baptism. These women are committed to standing against the tide of clerical oppression by:

— writing and speaking for equal rights in the church;
— withdrawing their financial support from oppressive pastors or bishops;
— joining women's church groups for support in the struggle;
— taking membership in the Women's Ordination Conference;
— studying for degrees to be ready for ordination and demanding equal salary for equal work in the church;

— rising up to protest unjust actions against women;

— raising other women's consciousness to the sins of patriarchy;

— giving other women voice by support and encouragement;

— financially supporting women who work for equality;

— teaching, counseling, mentoring, collaborating, companioning, supporting, listening to, and empowering other women whenever and wherever
possible.

Individual women from across the United States gave testimony to their efforts
to reclaim their rightful place in the chosen race, the royal priesthood, the holy
nation of God's own people:

> I have to remind myself that I oppress myself. I need education. I have to
> remind myself that my ministry is not limited to what I was taught. I am a cer-
> tified Catholic chaplain. I have to be creative and not break the rules, but
> some rules I impose on myself. I am trying to free myself from those bonds.
> [Married Woman, Virginia]

> I encourage women to stand up for themselves, not to be intimidated by the
> system. I speak out on their behalf whenever possible. [Single Woman, Texas]

> I encourage women to go for training and to risk by challenging the clergy so
> they might be able to use their natural leadership ability. [Sister, New York]

> I work to help women realize they are in oppressive situations and present
> alternative behavior to manifest their belief that there should be equality.
> [Widow, Ohio]

In the face of centuries of clerical domination, these individual examples of
women's efforts, notable as they are, by themselves cannot dislodge patriarchy.
While it is important to encourage and applaud grassroots women's attempts
to shed the shackles of patriarchy, a much more concerted and forceful
approach is needed. All justice-seeking women must engage in a concentrated,
consciousness-raising effort.

> We have to take our struggle for justice in the church so seriously that we will
> use every single opportunity to make people aware of the sexism that exists
> in the church. Initially we might feel embarrassed, but soon we will realize
> that our consciousness-raising efforts are moments of affirmation for our-
> selves, women who are made in the image and likeness of God.[20]

Where can women look for that maturity, courage, and strength to trans-
form the church and remain in it? Who better to give women courage than

Mary, the mother of Jesus? Contrary to the submissive, passive, docile woman presented to us throughout church history, women Scripture scholars envision Mary very differently today. They see her as a woman of faith and intelligence, decisive, strong, and courageous. One who could make great sacrifices and was willing to risk in order to do the right thing. She had no blueprint to guide her in her role and was certainly walking a road no one had walked before, but she believed in herself as well as in her God.

Life in the twentieth century is exceedingly more complicated than it was in Mary's time. The patriarchal system, divisive, oppressive, and complex, divides woman today and no woman could ever begin to change it alone. In addition to being faith-filled, women also need to look to feminist mentors and theologians who have studied patriarchy to give them direction and practical suggestions.

Carolyn Osiek, RSCJ, observes that there is an urgent need to work for the transformation of structures through the transformation of consciousness. She offers three ways for doing this:

> The first is to claim women's history and spiritual traditions. . . . Get to know the wonderful women of our tradition and our present: leaders of prayer, scholars, missionaries, and pastoral workers.
>
> Second, affirm women's goodness. . . . The silence of women is not so much men's fault as the women's who are unable or unwilling to have similar confidence in themselves.
>
> Third, do what can be done within present limits. . . . Women must become theologically educated, engage in Bible study and prayer groups, become comfortable with women as leaders of prayer, pastoring and critical thought.[21]

Elizabeth Schüssler Fiorenza speaks to women regarding the necessity of overcoming various divisions in order to come together to form a new church:

> These patriarchal divisions and competitions among women must be transformed into a movement of women as people of God. Feminist biblical spirituality must be incarnated in a historical movement of women struggling for liberation. It must be lived in prophetic commitment, compassionate solidarity, consistent resistance, affirmative celebration, and in grassroots organizations of the ekklesia of women.[22]

Theologian Regina Coll, CSJ, shared her concern about the future both for herself and for others who are committed to the feminist movement.

I hope I am always open, I don't think feminism is the final answer. I think it is an improvement, a step, but when somebody breaks through to the next resurrection theme, I don't want to say, no, I know what the truth is, I've already found it.[23]

Susan Muto shared similar ideas when she warned women that if they find themselves in a posture of rigidity toward other's ideas, it is time to examine their attitude. "That kind of self-examination," she noted, "may be a start in overcoming the devastating problem of women putting other women down."[24]

In the first national gathering of woman-church in 1983, Rosemary Radford Ruether defined feminist women as an exodus community coming out of exile, seeking liberation from patriarchy.

> We must do more than protest against the old. We must begin to live the new humanity now. We must begin to incarnate the community of faith in the liberation of humanity from patriarchy in words and deed, in new words, new prayers, new symbols, and new praxis. This means that we need to form gathered communities to support us as we set out on our exodus from patriarchy.[25]

Ruether's challenge is already almost fifteen years old, and women have not yet crossed the Red Sea in their exodus from patriarchy. They have formed some gathered communities, but not all are in support of the journey. She questions whether

> those who have deep faith and courage of their convictions, both men and women who have caught an alternative vision of the church, will be able to communicate, to organize, and to sustain an authentic understanding of the true vision of Christ, the true spirit of the good news, as one in which we are all transformed into a community of mutual flourishing.[24]

The question that Ruether poses today must be answered with action. As followers of Jesus, each of us is called to imitate his inclusivity, to respond to his plea for unity and to work for justice and peace. For women, this has a particular meaning: We must find our voice, we must dare to speak. Certainly, ours is a monumental task requiring great sacrifice and tireless labor. It may cost us dearly, but it will set us free from oppression.

> How are we to reclaim for the people [women] what has been until now the privilege of a few? . . . We [must] look at the present without ignoring its

shackles. We [must also] look toward the future without ignoring its cost. But if we really want to become a people of equals, our commitment as women will be toward eliminating any kind of discriminatory activity.[27]

Can we call ourselves Christians if we ignore this challenge?

NOTES

1. Lois W. Banner, *Elizabeth Cady Stanton: A Radical for Women's Rights,* Oscar Handlin, ed. (Boston: Little Brown and Company, 1980), 157.

2. Tama Starr, comp., *The Natural Inferiority of Women: Outrageous Pronouncements by Misguided Males* (New York: Poseidon Press, 1991), 44.

3. Giuseppe Beschin, trans., *La Trinita* (Rome: Citta Nuova Editrice, 1973), 476: 12.7.10.

4. Emmanuel D'Lorenzo, O.M.I., *Sacrament of Orders* as quoted in "Does the Church Discriminate Against Women on the Basis of Their Sex?" by Catherine Beaton, *Critic* (June-July 1966): 21–27.

5. *The New Testament of the Inclusive Language Bible,* Gal.3:28, Notre Dame, Ind: Cross Cultural Publications, Cross Roads Books, 1994.

6. English translation of the *Catechism of the Catholic Church* for the United States of America, United States Catholic Conference, Inc.-Libreria Editrice Vaticana, 1994, 324.

7. *Saint Joseph Baltimore Catechism,* Official Revised Edition No. 2 (New York: Catholic Book Publishing Company, 1969), 149.

8. Document from the Bishops' Committee on Women in Society and in the Church. Quoted in the *Pittsburgh Post-Gazette,* 11 October 1994, A-3.

9. Michael Crosby, OFM, *Spirituality of the Beatitudes* (Maryknoll, NY: Orbis Books, 1981), 202.

10. Mary Collins, interview, March 1994.

11. See Francis Bernard O'Connor, *Like Bread Their Voices Rise* (Notre Dame, Ind.: Ave Maria Press, 1993) and accompanying video *Crumbs From the Table.*

12. Rosemary Radford Ruether, "Can Women Stay in the Church?" *CHURCHWATCH,* August-September, 1994, 7.

13. Amanda Smith, "Most Women Want to Share Power, not Dominate Men," *South Bend Tribune,* 5 December 1993, F2.

14. Ruether, "Can Women Stay in the Church?," 7.

15. Judith Plaskow, *Standing Again at Sinai* (San Francisco: Harper & Row, 1990) 127.

16. Sandra M. Schneiders, IHM, *Beyond Patching: Faith and Feminism in the Catholic Church* (New York: Paulist Press, 1991), 5.

17. Ibid, 15.

18. Paulo Freire, *Pedagogy of the Oppressed* (New York: Continuum, 1993), 27.

19. Eileen McKeown, CSJ, interview, April 1994.

20. Ada Maria Isasi-Diaz, "A Mujerista Perspective on the Future of the Women's Movement and the Church," in *Defecting in Place,* Miriam Therese Winter, Adair Lummis, and Allison Stokes, (New York: Crossroad, 1994), 233.

21. Carolyn Osiek, RCSJ, "Women in the Church: Where Do We Go From Here?," *New Women New Church,* 16/17, nos. 6, 1–3, (1993/1994): 17

22. Elizabeth Schüssler Fiorenza, *In Memory of Her: A Feminist Theological Reconstruction of Christian Origins,* (New York: Crossroad, 1983), 349.

23. Regina Coll, CSJ, interview, February 1994.

24. Susan Muto, interview, April 1994.

25. Rosemary Radford Ruether, *Women-Church: Theory and Practice,* (San Francisco:Harper and Row, 1985), 5.

26. Rosemary Radford Ruether, "Can Women Stay in the Church?", 7.

27. Virginia Fabella and Mercy Amba Oduyoye, ed., *With Passion and Compassion: Third World Women Doing Theology* (Maryknoll, N.Y.: Orbis Books, 1989), 158.

PART II
THE FACES OF BRAZILIAN WOMEN

If women are the majority in the church, the majority of pastoral agents, then why does the clerical, patriarchal church flourish? What are women doing to collaborate with patriarchy?

Ana Flora Anderson
Interview, February 1995

Chapter 8

HOPE IN THE MIDST OF HEARTACHE

Any institution that accepts patriarchy as its model and patriarchal images as its symbols and its vision will have little credibility in the process of building a just and equal society.[1]

Beginning in the 1960s the growth of the "Communidades de Base" (Base Communities or CEBs)[2] in Brazil's interior and the periphery of its large cities has given hope to Catholic women. Because the majority of men view church attendance as "women's role," women predominate in leading the community in prayer as well as in addressing social issues. This has given them a sense of value in a machistic, patriarchal church and society.

In the early 1990s women interviewed spoke with excitement and enthusiasm about the future of the CEBs and their vision of a new kind of church in which women would have an equal place.

The community supports each person, welcomes and values you. You have more liberty in the CEB and they try to live the gospel that everyone is equal. If you have a problem, the community hears you. You learn a lot, and each day you discover God in different ways.[3]

Today, the mood is very different. For the most part, women are pessimistic about the future of the CEBs. One charter member of a CEB spoke of both her frustration and her determination:

There are just a few of us women who are stubborn enough to keep struggling to bring the life of the people in the community. There is no longer any incentive or enthusiasm. The priest doesn't care. If we want to do something we can but the priest doesn't encourage us. That's why we are called dinosaurs, because we refuse to have our spines broken by the issues and the struggle ahead. [Middle-Aged Married Woman, São Paulo]

In São Paulo, the spokesperson for a group of women whose CEB has been dormant for a couple of years had this to say:

> What we are feeling in the community is that things have stopped. Before we were so enthusiastic and anxious to do anything, get a course in theology and learn to become more active. . . . We have had two priests who cut out a lot of things everyone was involved and interested in. All of a sudden people feel they are not respected or valued, put to the side and told to stop what they are doing. [Older Woman, São Paulo]

She concluded by saying, "We are feeling a lot of confusion; why should we struggle? This is true especially when the priest tells us the church is only for praying, not for addressing social issues."

Many women in Brazil, theologians, philosophers, and educators among them, believe there is a concerted effort taking place on the part of the institutional church to dilute the power of the Brazilian CEBs, which have been heralded as the hope of the church of the future.

"It's not a Conciliar vision of church open to the world," says theologian Ivone Gebara, "but one of domination. Since the church isn't able to dialogue, it dominates by force—closing in on the people and intellectuals, like any other dictatorial regime."[4]

A major superior of sisters corroborated Gebara's theory. "I was in Rome recently with Carlos Mesters and he was telling me that Rome is fearful of the project 'Palavra Vida' (Word of Life) because it is putting the gospel into the hands of the people." She also noted, "Reading and reflecting on God's word is how we grow and begin to see how God walks with God's people, and how we can develop as strong women." [Sister, Paraná]

> Perhaps the most worrisome development in the Latin American church is a pre-Vatican II mentality among the younger clergy," said Chilean liberation theologian Ronaldo Muñoz. This new wave of conservative clericalism has brought with it strategies to contain Christian base communities, small grassroots faith groups that become one of the backbones of a new model of church and a principal expression of liberation theology.[5]

When almost two hundred Brazilian women were interviewed about their ecclesial reality, examples of and reference to "clerical control," "power," "fear," and "divisiveness" surfaced frequently. As early as 1983, theologian Leonardo Boff posed the question: "Who is afraid of the Base Ecclesial Communities?" He answers:

All of us who have difficulty in climbing down from our pedestal and placing ourselves in a position of humble listening to the voice of those who historically had no voice and through whom today we receive the great questioning of our consciences and an opportunity for conversion.[6]

Since the CEBs are composed primarily of women, and women are the leaders and animators, the suspicion is that the hierarchical church fears this new power of women. Frances O'Gorman has worked in Rio de Janeiro with the CEBs for many years and concludes otherwise:

I wouldn't say that the church fears the feminine aspect of the base communities, but it fears losing control. It's the control that scares them. Women have always done all the work. They're not afraid of the women; they are afraid of losing their clerical control when women start baking bread and sharing eucharist.[7]

O'Gorman expressed her own disillusionment with the CEBs. She described them not just as worshipping communities but also as communities seeking social change. She pointed out that while these communities have influenced many to work for change, they have not addressed the cause of the problems. "All the talk about the CEBs as the new church, the church on the move," she said, "hasn't made a difference as far as the institutional church is concerned, so they are to be questioned."

One of the strategies used against the CEBs is division. In 1989 the Vatican divided the progressive archdiocese of São Paulo into five small dioceses and appointed very conservative bishops, some of whom belong to "Opus Dei." This diffused the power and influence of both the CEBs and the visionary Paulo Evaristo Cardinal Arns. New parishes were formed that cut across and divided former parishes and small communities, dispersing the power of the people who had worked and prayed together for a quarter of a century. "This strategy was on purpose," noted one woman,

Our CEBs were a power house. Those in power were afraid of us. They were afraid that if we continued something would really happen. A whole new thing was coming to birth. In order to stop all of that we were divided and the CEBs almost no longer exist. The church has power, and she is the one who gives but also takes away. [Widow, São Paulo]

Ivone Gebara shared her insights regarding the actions of the church:

I believe the center of the problem is a vision of the world, of humanity and of the role of the church. I think that the institutional church, not the church as people of God but the hierarchical church, is afraid of the world. This is the typical behavior of someone who is afraid—the fearful one attacks, protects herself or himself, uses prisons for those who think differently. The fearful one does not dialogue.[8]

"The CEBs are becoming a minority," said a sister who had been working with them in São Paulo for more than twenty years. "There are not many being born and a lot are disappearing. Diocesan planning is diluting and interfering with the power and influence of the CEBs." Her sentiments were echoed by theologian Tereza Cavalcanti, who described another means the institutional church is using to undercut the CEBs:

The charismatic renewal communities, which have been accepted by the official church, highly value the whole clerical system, priests, bishops and pope. Even though they don't pay attention to the laws on sexuality, they highly regard the sacramental system. Some people are leaving the CEBs and going to the charismatic communities. Those who stay in the CEBs are experiencing a loss of hope, almost desperation.[9]

Franciscan Sister Silvia Regina de Lima Silva, a theology student at the Pontifical University in Rio, spoke of the influence the CEBs still have in the Brazilian church:

The communities are becoming a place of a different kind of power than the power the traditional church has always held. And the Vatican perceives this. It sees the journey of the Latin American church and recognizes that Rome isn't the center of the world! God is revealed in other places.

She then explained more about the source of the Vatican's anxiety.

This is a displacement. The presence and revelation of the Spirit don't have a fixed place. The Spirit blows where it will—not just in the magisterium, but in the midst of the people. This is the source of much conflict.[10]

The women in today's Brazilian society view life differently from those who struggled through the twenty years (1964–85) of the previous government dictatorship.[11] Even though young women have heard of the pain and difficulties their predecessors experienced, they do not feel the same urgency to become involved. "We were motivated because of the dangers we saw around us," said one of the old-timers, but "women today don't have the same motivation." Bonding together in the CEBs, with the help of the church, women managed to resolve many problems relating to their basic needs. "Today, when we start talking politics, when we see an arena for getting other kinds of rights, the church withdraws its support," noted another member of the group. Women believe the church is not willing to stand by them should anything happen; they feel alone. A third woman remarked, "The voice that was so strong for such a long time, the voice of the church for the poor and those struggling for their rights, has dropped into the background."

One reason Brazilian women today are not eagerly joining the struggle for justice and equality is that so many now work outside the home. Previously, women had more time to sit, talk, reflect, and question together. Today, even with their husbands' salaries, they still struggle financially. The women have to work, they are tired, and they have no time to participate in a CEB.

Those who have been involved in the struggle for twenty or thirty years are also tired. They are tired of the struggle. "There is a terrible exhaustion that comes from this kind of work," a sister pointed out. "That's the price of being a prophet."

"The old mentality still exists among some women today," said one woman, "that to go to church is only to go and pray, not to get involved in anything. Go and find peace for your soul, leave your problems there. To get involved in any social issues, is not the kind of church they want," she said. "It scares them and they back off and don't want to get involved."

What has changed hope to heartache for many women in Brazil is the price of being prophets, the lack of energy on the part of the younger generation of women to carry on the struggle, the timidity and selfishness of those who do not want to get involved, the moral decay and power struggle of so many of the clergy, and the increase of "Opus Dei" bishops and priests who are closing off the lifeline of the people in the CEBs.

Ana Flora Anderson, who has taught theology to seminarians for many years, admitted that she is concerned about the quality of seminarians because they are becoming more and more conservative and rigid. Also, in contrasting the years of liberation theology with the present, she pointed out that the option for the poor, which was previously the focus of all the courses, has now disappeared. "There is nothing life-giving or exciting today," she said. "Neither the professors nor the students refer to the poor anymore." Also, she said, nearly half the seminarians are gay, and often flaunt it. Many are dying of AIDS. According to Anderson, gay seminarians see women students as a threat, as competition for the other men. "The best students," she said, "were those of fifteen years ago."[12]

Anderson anguished, "Ever since you phoned me for this interview, I've been thinking about what I was going to say. What have I done all these years? Some part of this must be my fault! Has it all been a waste?"

Why did she blame herself? She could have attributed the deplorable status of the seminarians and the church to such factors as the oppression by the Vatican, the new "Opus Dei" bishops, the Roman influence on young students, the lack of commitment of the seminary authorities, or the poor curriculum. One has to wonder where her male counterparts would have assigned the blame.

This self-oppression that women of all classes and professions continue to inflict on themselves, along with the poor self-image patriarchal conditioning imposes on women, was clearly identifiable when Anderson related how amazed she was, after thirty-five years, to read in the paper that she was cited as one of Brazil's leading women theologians. The article had been written by a male theologian and she realized that she still needed affirmation from men to help her believe what she already knew about herself!

At this point in the interview we were joined by Marguerite Olivia, professor of religious studies, and Sonia, one of Anderson's former students, a biblicist and a woman religious. The discussion shifted to the question of women and their priestly baptismal role and the potentiality of women as ordained priests.

Sonia posed the first question: "In what way do we women really live our priestly role in the world today? We cannot just be servants of the priest, we must have a definite role."[13]

Other issues also concerned Anderson. "Since we have all been baptized into the priesthood of Christ, how do we as women act out our priesthood in a way that does not fortify the clerical priesthood that exists? It is very important," she said, "that we as women see how we should be priestly without reinforcing and reproducing the horrible things we have seen among the clerical priesthood." Anderson then declared emphatically, "Women, instead of wanting to be priests, should pull the whole thing down. We would only give them consolation and strengthen the system if we joined them."

Olivia agreed with Anderson that the answer is not to ordain women, but to get the assembly to celebrate Eucharist together.

> That's the way we will have a new church. That's the only way to get rid of clericalism. That's the way the grassroots can do it. When we have the conviction that it is the assembly together that consecrates, we will start celebrating without priests in small groups.[14]

Olivia continued, "I belong to a small group like this. The church will always try to control this and keep the power, not thinking of power as a service." With the wisdom of the elderly she added, "The change will come from the grassroots, and it is happening slowly."

But with the scarcity of priestly vocations today and the fact that many who are ordained either leave after a few years or die of AIDS, Olivia noted, "Women won't have to pull it down. It is going to finish by itself."

The hopes of women for more space in their church are continually plagued by the institutional church's ongoing efforts to dominate and control them. However, Ivone Gebara gives much needed support to their hope when she describes the growing strength of women in Brazil.

> Women's ministry is shaking up men's ministry, challenging their practice and the exercise of their authority. This is taking place, not because of some decision taken by women to make it happen, but because of the nature and quality of their service and of the new social role that they are winning in the world.[15]

Perhaps it is not a question of hope or heartache but rather a struggle to maintain hope in the midst of heartache. One woman who experienced betrayal by a priest, who preached liberation and denounced violence against women, summed it up well when she said,

> After that, I said I'd never work directly with a priest again. Yes, with the people. Yes, with the church (community). But with priests, no. Not without their true support. Not unless they truly respect laypeople and women. . . . This will only change when we demand respect and dignity.[16]

Notes

1. Ranjani Rebara, "Challenging Patriarchy," in *Feminist Theology from the Third World*, ed. Ursula King, (Maryknoll, N.Y.: Orbis Books, 1994), 109.
2. Robert S. Pelton, CSC, *From Power to Communion: Toward a New Way of Being Church Based on the Latin American Experience* (Notre Dame, Ind.: University of Notre Dame Press, 1994), xv; Frances O'Gorman, *Base Communities in Brazil* (Ventnor, N.J.: Overseas Ministries Study Center, 1983), 30.
3. Frances Bernard O'Connor, *Like Bread Their Voices Rise: Global Women Challenge the Church* (Notre Dame, Ind.: Ave Maria Press, 1993), 126.
4. Ivone Gebara in *The Struggle is One*, ed. Mev Puleo, (Albany: SUNY Press, 1994), 214.

5. David Molineaux, "Women, Native People Challenge Theology," *National Catholic Reporter,* 15 September 1995, 12.

6. Leonardo Boff, "Qem tem Medo da Igreja Popular?" in *Revista de Cultra Vozes*, no. 4 (May 1983): 64.

7. Frances O'Gorman, interview, March 1995.

8. Gebara in *The Struggle Is One*, 214–15.

9. Tereza Maria Cavalcanti, interview, February 1995.

10. Sylvia Regina de Lima Silva in *The Struggle Is One*, ed. Mev Puleo, (Albany: SUNY Press, 1994), 103.

11. Castelio Branco, 1964–67; Artur da Costa e Silva, 1967–69; Emilio Garrastazu Medici, 1969–74; Ernesto Geisel, 1974–78; Joao Baptista Figueiredo, 1978–85.

12. Anderson, interview.

13. Sonia, interview, February 1995.

14. Marguerite Olivia, interview, February 1995.

15. Ivone Gebara, "Women Doing Theology in Latin America" in *Feminist Theology From the Third World*, ed. Ursula King, (Maryknoll, N.Y.: Orbis Books, 1994), 58–59.

16. Goreth Barradas, in *The Struggle Is One*, ed. Mev Puleo, (Albany: SUNY Press, 1994), 51.

Chapter 9

IN GOD'S IMAGE?

The active involvement of women in the church can only be a reality when women are seen as real people, created in God's image.[1]

In his apostolic letter *On the Dignity of Women* Pope John Paul II states clearly that "the human being—man and woman—has been created in God's image."[2] If the official church holds this to be true, why do so many women feel they are second-class members of their church? Because historically they have been programmed to believe they are inferior. St. Paul and the early church fathers, along with Thomas Aquinas in the middle ages, were largely responsible, not just for questioning whether women were made in God's image, but in fact, for betraying them by denying that they are. In his first letter to the Corinthians, 11:6–7, Paul wrote:

If a woman will not wear a veil, she ought to cut off her hair. If it is shameful for a woman to have her hair cut off, or her head shaved, it is clear that she ought to wear a veil. A man, on the other hand, ought not to cover his head, because he is the image of God and the reflection of his [God's] glory. Woman, in turn, is the reflection of man's glory.

In the Middle Ages Thomas Aquinas, influenced by Aristotle's thinking, taught that the male was created with superior capacity for knowledge and with a rational soul, whereas the female was created chiefly as an aid in reproduction. Aquinas referred to women as "misbegotten males, necessary to the continuation of the human race, but certainly inferior to men."[3] Aquinas's teachings were the "bible" for theologians up to and through Vatican II. So it is not any wonder that women's struggle to gain a credible image has been so difficult.

Long after the close of Vatican II, Pope Paul VI in his famous 1976 encyclical "Inter Insigniores" spoke of women's incapacity to image Christ as the

85

major obstacle to the ministerial priesthood. This document formed the basis for John Paul II's letter in 1994 declaring the church's inability to ordain women to the priesthood. Yet popes and bishops alike repeatedly protest that women and men are equal human beings. As recently as 1995, in *A Letter to Women*, John Paul II described Jesus' attitude toward women:

> When it comes to setting women free from every kind of exploitation and domination, the gospel contains an ever relevant message which goes back to the attitude of Jesus Christ himself. Transcending the established norms of his own culture, Jesus treated women with openness, respect, acceptance and tenderness. In this way he honored the dignity which women have always possessed according to God's plan and in God's love.[4]

The pope goes on to pose a very important question. He asks, "as we look to Christ at the end of this second millennium, it is natural to ask ourselves *how much of his message has been heard and acted upon?*"

In order to formulate an answer to John Paul's question, two additional questions must be posed: What was Jesus' message for women and how have the practices, policies, and writings of the church fulfilled that message for women?

It would simplify our task if we could open the New Testament to the chapter and verse where Jesus reveals his message for women, but he did not teach that way. All of his messages were presented as parables, metaphors, or stories, as well as in his own example. Frequently in Scripture Jesus said to his disciples, "do you still not understand?" Many of his teachings were unclear to them as well. Perhaps it is not surprising that the patriarchal church, in all these hundreds of years, still has not understood the message of Jesus for women. As one woman from the interior of Brazil noted, "If the church truly believes in the example of Jesus, it should be the first to accept women as full and equal participants. The Catholic Church, however, has not and does not even today, view women as Jesus did."

Frances O'Gorman, aware of the deceptive messages women receive from the patriarchal church, provided additional insights into the twofold struggle many Brazilian women are waging to achieve some semblance of recognition in society and the church. "The Brazilian culture," she said, "was formed within the Catholic Church, a reality very different from that of North America."[5]

In O'Gorman's view, the paternalistic church did not simply support the injustice and oppression of women in the indigenous culture but actually blessed this oppression by supporting the machistic society as well:

From childhood women accept abnegation and masochism, and learn submissive forms of behavior. . . . In our society machismo is considered to be a
legacy of the past, inherited from both the indigenous society and the
Portuguese conquerors. Women experience fatalistically the brutality and
power of men. For years and years they endure the physical and psychological punishment from their husbands, brothers and fathers. Women have come
to consider themselves second-class people with no rights. They behave like
minors who ask permission for everything.[6]

No wonder so many women have no idea how to extricate themselves from
their submissive state.

A Brazilian sister explained why she feels some women embrace a submissive place in the church. She said, "Inside the church women's acceptance is
even more complete because of the sacred space that is deep inside all of us."
To these women the priest is the symbol of the Sacred. Women whose husbands are unfaithful and/or abusive seek solace from their priest, who is celibate and educated. They revere him, and want to serve him. "This is fulfilling
to them," added another sister.

Some sisters also deify the clergy. Since they cannot be priests, they feel that
if they serve them, they will come closer to the Sacred. That is why so many
sisters are happy to wait on the clergy.

The sacramental system is an instrument of power and control used by the
hierarchy. Women, who comprise the vast majority of members in the CEBs,
are submissive to the priest when he comes because he brings the sacraments,
baptism for their children and a blessing on their marriages and their dead.
The clerical church holds power over their life and death. Women are afraid to
speak up for more because they do not want to lose the comfort of the sacraments. As long as access to the sacraments is tied to a clerical power base,
women are caught in the system and very few will sever that lifeline.

Most Brazilian women seem to be united in the view of the clergy as the dei-
fied male model. They have been taught, like women everywhere in the
Catholic world, that because Jesus only chose men as his apostles, the only
ones who can celebrate Eucharist are duly ordained male ministers. So if a
woman cannot be ordained, if the Vatican says there is something wrong with
women wanting to be priests, then she has no right to aspire to a ministry that
is reserved to men.

"The difficulty in the church for women," noted Irma Passoni, former religious and political activist, "is that they have been taught that God is male,
therefore males in the persons of their fathers, husbands, brothers and sons are
images of God and the woman has to be submissive to this vision."[7] This has

a profound impact on women and most find it difficult to challenge. Her thinking echoes Mary Daly's "If God is male then the male is God."[8]

"This masculine image of God," a sister theologian pointed out, "is the root of women's problem. If the image of God is male, then it's the man who's going to save me, pardon my sins and lead the Eucharist." She noted, "It doesn't make any difference whether the priest or bishop is conservative or not, the problem is with us women." When a sister theologian planned an Ash Wednesday service without a priest, the sisters participated, told her how lovely it was, and then went out to a "regular" Mass. "It is the same with the other women," she said. "We have this need for the sacraments and right now men are the only ones who can administer them, so we have no choice."[9] On the other hand there are women in some CEBs who, after becoming accustomed to sisters presiding at their weekly communion service, indicate they prefer "sister's Mass" to father's.

The thinking that equates the male with the sacraments is so strong that even when women have the opportunity, as in the Methodist Church, to receive the sacraments from a woman, they often refuse to do so. A Methodist pastor in a rural community still recalls the pain of her first experience in ministry. She stood alone at the altar with the bread and wine, and the people refused to receive it from her. "It is all right for you to lead the prayer, but to give me the Eucharist or to baptize my son, I need a man," said one woman. They expected her to do all the women's roles, play the piano, fix the flowers, clean the church, do the laundry. However, the women, in particular, refused to accept her as pastor.

When another woman met with a conference of Methodist women to learn why they had rejected her as their minister, they said, "The men are the image of God, they always know more than the women!" Many women learned well the lessons of patriarchy and continue to criticize and ostracize other women for not staying in their place. These women believe wanting to be a priest or minister is not the proper role for women. "An attractive unmarried woman standing in front of a congregation cannot help but call attention to herself. If she wants to be accepted, she is forced to downplay her femininity and act more like a man, the only acceptable model."[10]

Two examples of how the male model or the father figure dominates the thinking of some Brazilian religious were related by a woman psychologist and a woman theologian:

> In the northeast of Brazil there are congregations of sisters founded by bishops for the sole purpose of taking care of them. The sisters clean their houses, do their secretarial work, and care for their every personal need. These are

groups of women who dedicate their lives, because of the need they have for a "father figure," to take care of the clergy. If this isn't sexual repression, I don't know what is![11]

When the Pope was here in São Paulo, he had a special meeting in a big gymnasium for all the religious of the city. The place was filled with nuns and I was watching it on TV. I was so ashamed because a Freudian would have lost her mind looking at the scene. The nuns were shouting his name, almost panting, putting their hands all over him. All I could think of was all that sexual repression coming out all over the figure of the pope. Most of the sisters were older women. This was a film that should be used in a meeting of religious so they could start asking themselves what is behind this kind of male idol worship and behavior. [12]

This deification of the male model and all that it represents accounts for the behavior of some women in positions of leadership in the CEBs. "In my CEB," recounted a young Brazilian sister, "there is a woman who is called the 'matriarch' of the community. Even the men are afraid of her. Whatever idea she suggests, happens." She pointed out that even though people complain, the "matriarch" uses the masculine model of force and reproduces the same system as the men. "This woman orders everyone around and everybody has to be quiet. She has adopted this model because it is the only one put before her. In order to retain power, she has to use it." Another sister indicated that women like this are not even aware they are dominating others. What they are doing is emulating priests or other women who embrace the patriarchal model.

"Whether it is in the church, politics or society, noted Irma Passoni, "we women replicate the male model. We don't create a feminine model. We do what everybody recognizes and accepts."[13]

Women have a theoretical awareness of what they are doing, but the process of putting it into practice is different and very difficult, because it requires changes in our way of being, and presupposes confrontation. Such confrontation is very difficult. A lot of times it's easier to let things go the way they are.[14]

Many women have a love/hate relationship not just with patriarchy but with machismo as well. The evidence of the hold machismo has on women is reflected in the responses to the question: "Do women, who suffer from the evils of machismo, try to change the system by raising their children in a different way?"

No, they may say something different, but when they actually have children they will go back to raising them the same way they were raised. Women perpetuate the system because society is machista. We were raised like that, our mothers were like that. I can raise my child differently, but he has to live in this society. I could lose my husband and my house and be discriminated against in my own family. [Woman in CEB, Paraná]

We carry within ourselves our own domination. We are afraid that other women will talk about us if we are different, if we do things against the social customs. It's easy to talk about other families, but in my own family I reproduce the same model. [Woman in Favela,[15] São Paulo]

Women, instead of getting together to change the system, reproduce it. They don't have an awareness, so they buy into it. It's much easier to go along with it than try to figure it out. [Teacher/Administrator]

A few women do have the courage to rebel against machismo. One educated woman in the state of Bahia spoke about how hard it was to train her sons in a manner that went against the machistic culture. "We mothers are the worst machistas," she said, "we are teachers of machismo. If we are not vigilant, we will train our girls to wash the plates and make the beds and let the boys run free." As she was speaking the door opened and her son, an architect, came out on the verandah carrying a tray of tea and cake for us. Her face broke into a broad smile. "Oh, I was hoping he would do this!" She had obviously been vigilant in the education of her sons.

There is, however, a price to pay for such behavior. When the question was posed: "Does consciousness raising in regard to machismo threaten marriages?" A woman from São Paulo responded:

Yes, it is a constant threat. I was married for thirty-five years and frequently during that time, my husband would put me up against the wall and say I had to choose between my struggle against machismo and him. He could not understand why I educated our sons and daughters to be equal and to see their work as equal. Finally, after thirty-five years, he left me.

Surprisingly, she was neither devastated nor full of regret:

I believe it was worth it. I look at my children today and can see what a difference it has made. My son is a bank manager, he comes home and makes dinner for the family. My other son and his wife worked with a group of people to build a house. When it came time to sign the papers for the house, because he hadn't worked as much as his wife, he had her sign the papers [unheard of in Brazil].

She concluded by saying with pride, "These are the fruits of my life." Then sadly, "Many women who have worked with me against machismo have separated from their husbands."

No one describes women's reality in the patriarchal church and machistic society of Brazil better than Maria Clara Bingemer:

> It is an indisputable fact that women carry on their shoulders a large part of the actual work of the church. In the base community and the parish, in the schools, movements and pastoral work, women, both nuns and lay women, are present as coordinators, catechists, enablers, giving of their best, their time, their warmth, their strength, their guts, their lives, even their blood. . . . In the church and in society women are struggling to conquer a space for themselves, affirming their incontestable leadership in the base communities, registering their presence in the popular movement, carrying out nearly all the important catechetical work, and entering at last into the field of work on theology and spirituality.[16]

And what is their reward? How are they appreciated for all their hard work and devoted service? "We have been taught," noted a woman from the interior, "that God created woman from the rib of man so that we could be equals and walk side by side. But, I think God created woman from the bottom of man's foot because we are constantly being stepped on."

"I know how it is in our church," said another woman involved in catechetical work. "If you are doing a work that's serving the people, they will use you. If you do anything that challenges the status quo, they'll throw you out."

Despite how they are viewed and treated, Catholic women do celebrate and are ministers of their celebrations. Women consecrate in the great celebrations that happen in their families when they cook beans, mix them with rice, and share with their children, husbands, and neighbors. This sharing of all that they have and are is the moment of consecration. "Jesus came and made himself bread, rice, and beans to be shared," said a young Brazilian sister, who worked as a domestic servant:

> This sharing brings smiles to the faces of children who have no school to go to, smiles to the women who work and fight to survive. It is the feast where we learn to put our feet strongly on the ground, to look pain straight in the face; to sing to the beauty of life, to learn to dance. It is where we learn to laugh at life each day. It is the celebration that consecrates, the sharing of the bread so that everybody has a piece. It is to believe and show that God is life! Deep down Brazilian women know they are created in God's image.

They know they are the backbone of their society and of their church. One woman passed mirrors around the group and said, "Look! The image you see is the image of God. You can only see God if you see beauty in yourself and the woman next to you."

What women are struggling for is recognition, and a clear and unambiguous acknowledgment on the part of the church that, whether they are single, widowed, divorced, separated, or sisters, they image God as fully and completely as men do.

NOTES

1. Lloyda Fanusie, "Women and the Church (Protestant)," paper presented at Port Harcourt, Nigeria, EATWOT Women's Commission, August 1986.
2. *Origins* 18, no. 17 (6 October 1988): 277.
3. *Summa Theologica,* 3a, qu.31, art.4.
4. Pope John Paul II, "A Letter to Women" in *The Tablet, International Catholic Weekly,* London, England, 15 July 1995, 917.
5. Frances O'Gorman, interview, March 1995.
6. "Gender and Ethnic Identity: an Overlooked Need," from Pablo Richard, "La iglesia que nace en America central," *Cristianismo y Sociedad,* no. 79, 1984.
7. Irma Passoni, interview, March 1995.
8. Mary Daly, *Beyond God the Father:Toward a Philosophy of Women's Liberation* (Boston: Beacon Press, 1973), 19.
9. Sister Marian, CDP, interview, March 1995.
10. Noemi, Brazilian Methodist minister, interview, March 1995.
11. Sister Marie Amelia, interview, February 1995.
12. Ana Flora Anderson, interview, February 1995.
13. Irma Passoni, interview, March 1995.
14. Ibid.
15. *Favelas,* usually described as "shantytowns," are squatter villages where people originally build homes out of any scrap materials they can find. Many people try to gradually improve their homes, adding firm walls and concrete floors, hoping to eventually obtain a legal title to the land they occupy. Mev Puleo, ed., *The Struggle Is One* (Albany: SUNY Press, 1994), 9
16. Maria Clara Bingemer, "De la teologia del laicado a la teologia del bautismo," *Paginas* 86 (1987): 9.

Chapter 10

VICTIMS OR PERPETRATORS?

Are we really such sinners or is it something that was put upon us throughout history?

Or, is this something we put on ourselves?[1]

The result of being born and reared in the macho-patriarchal world of Brazil was very evident in the conversations of both sisters and other women. They spoke about their own struggles and some of their successes and failures in their efforts to raise the consciousness of other women. They spoke about their formation in a patriarchal church and the crippling conditioning of their macho culture.

In many groups the pros and cons of the type of education given to women were debated. The focus was on how education has been used as a weapon against women: teaching them that they have no worth; depriving some of ever discovering what it means to be a woman; exposing them to fragmented ideas so that with naive consciousness they continue to promote what their mothers and grandmothers told them; instructing them to be submissive and therefore incapable of independent thought or actions.

Others claimed education as their lifeline. It opened the door to understanding and knowledge. Once their consciousness was raised, they began to value themselves and adhere to a new way of doing things.

"The way we are educated," said one woman, "is what represses or liberates us." She shared her experience of being educated at the hands of Catholic sisters:

I was always in trouble, made to stand in front of the class because I was an extrovert and very active. I was continually humiliated by the sisters, "Girls don't speak in loud voices, they don't dress that way, etc." I feared doing things because I was told that God would open up a hole and swallow me up. I had nightmares about the devil coming to get me because "the devil takes people who do things like I did." It was only as I matured and got help from another woman that I was able to work it out.

Another woman related similar experiences she had in a Catholic school. She, too, asked questions: "Why can't girls serve on the altar like boys? Why can't the sisters give Holy Communion like the priest?" She loved to dance and sing and the response from the sisters was always, "You are a daughter of the devil!" "At that time of my life," she said, "I felt very badly about religion because I saw that boys could do all they wanted to do and I couldn't because I was a 'daughter of the devil.'"

A member of a group of women factory workers in the center of the city of São Paulo observed, "Women's oppressive behavior is due to the education given to them in Brazil."

> They are educated to bow to men. Many times the only place they can be more or better is with their women friends. In their own base communities they oppress the other women because it's the only place they are valued or feel they are somebody, the only place they have any power. So they take advantage of it and just repeat the authoritative behavior of men.

One woman emphasized that this behavior is seen not just in the CEBs, but exists everywhere, particularly in the workplace. It is incorporated into women's identities through television propaganda and job training. "Many women oppress because they are brainwashed; it's not consciously done," she observed.

Others related how their own consciousness was raised to the oppressive effects of their ongoing education that the male is the only norm. One factory worker who had entered the work world early to support her family realized that through her discussions with women she began to see that being "machona" (a masculinized woman) was not what she wanted. "A woman can be strong without becoming a man," she concluded.

Another told of how she came to recognize that she herself was an oppressor of women. A supervisor of women in a factory, she was modeling autocratic leadership, forcibly suppressing all opposition in the same manner as her male colleagues. She then expressed her sorrow and told her colleagues she was working hard to move out of that model. However, another was quick to add, "Once your consciousness is raised, you are considered a dangerous element among the other workers who are not yet aware." Many of the women in this group spoke from experience, having been fired from previous jobs because of their strong stand for women's rights.

Maria Luiza Guedes Costa observed that when women become aware and begin questioning their own way of reproducing the male model of machismo, a conflict arises in their work with women who tend to protect men. She pointed out, "Some women make men infantile, they are mothers to them, while some men make women infantile in another way because they want to protect them."[2] Whether intended or not, the motivation is power and control. Women need to understand the danger of reproducing the male model because power and control are so destructive when misused.

In their homes as well as in the CEBs, women are slowly becoming aware of the debilitating effects of the machistic-patriarchal atmosphere into which they have been born. However, many are still pulled in two directions. The old ways die hard. In the early part of her marriage, one Brazilian woman said she was like any other woman in the way she was training her boys. She wanted them to be macho and thought they were cute when they acted that way. Later, because of her participation in the women's pastoral and discussion groups (a new form of education), she realized the harm she was doing and began to change her way of training her boys. Trying to make her teaching practical, she would point out the times they were upset at their father for not helping her. Then she would ask, "Are you going to be like him when you get married?" Yet, she admitted, if her sons got married she would be upset to find them in the kitchen doing dishes! Her reason: They are "my sons" and should be manly. If they were someone else's sons, she would think it acceptable. This woman concluded:

> There is still an awful lot women have to learn. From this discussion I can understand how much women are still oppressors of other women, without even knowing it. I feel this type of sharing is very important for us to be able to change our mentality and our actions.

A woman theologian described some benefits women receive from participating in the base communities.

> In the small communities women are recognized as people. They can leave the kitchen and the stove. They learn how to speak up and their words have power. In the circle everybody has a chance to talk. A lot of women used to keep their heads down and defer to men. They slowly came to perceive themselves as women capable of speaking, so they started to speak. They learn how to coordinate and confront. They see their own potential. They discover themselves in the process but there are a lot of vulnerable women who can't do this yet.[3]

A Methodist minister spoke of her efforts to raise women's consciousness to the fact that they have a right to participate simply because they are persons. "We are trying to make women aware of their equality with men in the church." She pointed out that traditional women do everything they can to stop this. They, in turn, oppress the women who are trying to bring about a new consciousness.

"It takes a long time to change history, but women are responsible for their own liberation. The struggle changes from hour to hour," observed one sister, "but it depends a lot on us. It will also depend on the men because there's no point in running up against the point of a knife. We have to convert them, too." This is the stumbling block in both the church and society. It is far more difficult for men to see any advantage in the liberation of women.

The realization that women must somehow convert men to an understanding of how women are oppressed and work with them to change the culture parallels the insights of Frances O'Gorman regarding the futility she feels about the efforts of the base communities over the past twenty-five years to change society and the institutional church:

> We have wanted the poor to change the church and the world. They don't have the capacity to do that; it's impossible. The causes are not among the poor, they are in the whole structure of society and the church. We have to work with the people who make the decisions.[4]

"The kind of structure women want for the church," she continued, "we can't get. We can't change it (because like the poor, we are powerless), so we end up adopting the male structure." She referred to the ordained women in the Methodist and Anglican churches who give it a feminine touch but adapt to the male structure. She went on to speak about the difficulties women have in standing free of their formation in the macho-patriarchal world of Brazil. "All of us have internalized the formation of the church," she said. "In the back of our minds we are still defending a papal, clerical church even though we know it oppresses us. It's hard to let that go because of our formation." She elaborated on the problem of living in a culture that was formed within the Catholic church. "We've mixed our spiritual values with our culture. The two are the same for many people and they find it difficult to separate them. We interpret some cultural practices as spiritual and the church capitalizes on that!"

"It's not just culture we inherit in life. Women must face up to their historical programming," noted Irma Passoni, former religious and political activist. "Our grandmothers and mothers had a certain guilt, which they passed on to us." She was speaking about a feeling of submission and unworthiness, expressed by telling girls they do not have a right to leisure but should be working all the time. She said, "The question is how to interrupt this guilt I inherited from my mother? It has to be interrupted! The majority of women don't know how to say 'no,' how to put limits." She concluded by affirming the importance of basic education, especially the training women receive in women's groups, where they learn they can be competent without diminishing the man.

Some of the best professionally educated women in Brazil are sisters, yet for many years their formation had a negative effect on them as women. A group of sister-formators in Bahia shared some of the debilitating ramifications of their own formation. They felt they were the victims and those who formed them were the perpetrators of their oppression.

> The whole question of our femininity was not just oppressed but repressed. This was exhibited in the way we dressed—wearing men's shoes, carrying men's umbrellas. We weren't men but we weren't women either. We were sort of neutral. We had our breasts bound so we wouldn't look like women and that was a castrating experience.

> Thirty years ago we received not just a habit but a formation we put on like a cloak, a spirituality that did not respect the personality development of the young sister. We had no way of growing as persons so there was no human formation.

> Friendship was something that was not permitted. When I was a novice I encountered the book by Francis de Sales called *Friendship and Love*. My novice mistress took it away from me when she saw me enjoying it. It was a great joy to me when Vatican II brought new meaning to friendship and the whole meaning of chastity in terms of friendship.

Two Dominican sisters, who had struggled with their communities to leave the institutional ministry and work with the poor, had strong opinions regarding the effects of religious formation on women.

> In regard to spiritual formation, we were caught up on forms of piety and even though that did produce holy women, it did not help us grow spiritually. The Bible was taken from our hands. We couldn't put our feet in the word of God and grow.

> Formation is to keep us dependent on the congregation. We nuns are often the most alienated of all women. I speak from my own reality of women in

Latin America. So many have fears and are not conscious of their dignity as women. The whole mental image of religious life has to change, it hasn't been touched yet. In recent years I discovered my identity with other groups of women outside the community.

A group of Brazilian sisters shared some of their feelings regarding their formation.

Women are formed to hang their heads. I saw this in my own home. The mother passes these ideas on in the family. There is no point in trying to change this. Since our mothers inculcated this idea in us, so in religious life when we encounter domination we allow ourselves to be dominated. It is a vicious circle. The big responsibility is the mother's. If she isn't aware of what she is doing then the children will carry it on. [Sister, Bahia]

A second sister offered a slightly different view. "I also think that religious life can wake women up to their own value." She explained that religious life was neither the cause of women's oppression nor their awareness.

It comes from what they have been educated or raised to believe. The essential point is the family, the way you were raised. Formation either helps you get more repressed or frees you more. It either reinforces what you had at home or opens places for new ideas.

She seemed to answer her own question of why it is that the same formation provides growth for some while crippling others.

Ivone Gebara added a new insight into the mystery of the formation of women religious. In an interview with author Mev Puleo, Gebara shared her concerns and wisdom:

For ten years now I have been very troubled by the things that oppress nuns religiously—they come from men. Men are the ones who impose certain behaviors. The blaming of the body comes from them.

I also began to notice that while women at the grassroots level were submissive, their submission wasn't as strong as that of the women religious.

Then I saw that everything was connected. Even economic poverty is linked with a patriarchal organization of society. I began to link religion with economy, with society, with psychology—how women think of themselves as less than men. Why? Why do people say, "What a shame that I had a daughter and not a son?"[5]

A religious community in Brazil, with progressive leadership, is grappling with yet another problem: understanding the younger generation. Post-Vatican II religious life values are interpreted differently by the young women entering their community today. "It is clear these values do not mean the same to the young as they do to us. We are losing our capacity to speak a language that is the same for all generations," noted the provincial superior. She shared an example of her frustration. The custom in her diocese was for each religious congregation to contribute to the diocesan seminary's scholarship fund. At the same time their own sisters, by obligation, work their way through college.

The provincial council decided the contribution was unjust since their own women had to work. The strongest reaction came from the young sisters, who challenged their decision. "God will not bless our work if we do this," the sisters said. "How can you deprive these young men of their education?" They had no thought for the injustice of the situation. "The young sisters," she said, "seem to have no desire to enter into a struggle for their rights." They prefer to stabilize things, keep them the way they are, the way they think they should be. They do not want new ideas or actions. "They live in front of a giant screen and watch the world go by as they criticize it. They don't seem to feel anything. This phenomenon," she said, "is too young to assess."

Perhaps these young sisters strongly believe the status quo for women in the church is God's will. It may not be that they are apathetic and unfeeling, as the provincial suggests, but that her position is not theirs.

Examples of women blindly following the commands of the clergy without struggling to discern the reality are legion. In the north, a childless woman who separated from her husband was told by the cardinal to take off all her jewelry and make-up, wear her hair in a bun, give everything to the diocese, and die to the world. She did what he asked without question, and gave her palatial house to the diocese for its use. The cardinal, in turn, put her name on it as the donor!

One example of a group's conditioned action involved a gathering of women religious who met with the Conference of Bishops to develop a sister-church project in the north of Brazil. The sisters prepared the "Sending Liturgy." When they arrived at the cathedral, there were seven men at the altar, including priests, bishops, and laymen, but not one woman. Five different talks were given, all by men. The point is not that the men took over, but that the women did not prepare any part for themselves. This lack did not even occur to them until they looked around at the six hundred women and realized that not a single word was spoken by even one of them. "The reason this happened," said one of the sisters, "is that we women have been conditioned to believe that the one who mediates the Sacred is the man. We don't even stop and reflect on it."

There is a great need for more sisters like Sonia, who asked: "Up to what point am I serving a church that tries to liberate people and one that is a machista church? In what way do we women really live our priestly role in the world today? We must not just be servants of the priests!"[6]

"There are women," noted one theologian, "that blindly follow what men in the church say. They conform immediately to the male scheme of things and don't struggle to discern."[7]

Another added, "as long as women continue to believe that they are not the companions of men but their servants, no change will come about."[8] "It's all caused by a lack of awareness," observed a sister. "Some women are neither equipped nor prepared to support other women or to speak up for themselves. We need more education to awareness." Until a significant number of women become convinced of their own equality, they will continue to actively participate in keeping all women powerless. In the interim, the patriarchal church and the machistic society will continue to capitalize on the large number of women who feed the system.

A key reason for women's inability to speak up for themselves was illustrated by a woman psychologist:

> There are women inside this structure who have never even questioned themselves yet about the patriarchy that surrounds them. They don't realize they carry the "father model" which has influenced them so strongly and which they continue to live and act in with no consciousness that there might be anything wrong with it.[9]

She clarified:

> There are two ways women act within this society. One is to become masculinized and carry out the masculine role along with the men in order to be valued. The other, to submit themselves totally to the desires and whims of the male figure whom they idolize.[10]

Since men, throughout history, have consistently been in the foreground, many women have been conditioned to believe that it is men's proper place. Today, as women come together more and their awareness is raised, some are awakening to their reality. One woman noted satirically, "In my community women have always had the 'last word.' The first word is that of the hierarchy, the second, the men's, and the last is given to the women as an afterthought."

Does the new generation of Brazilian women see things differently? It was noted in chapter 8 that younger women do not have the same motivation to work in the CEBs as did women thirty years ago. They are content to leave the struggle to others. In this chapter, we see that many young women entering religious communities today continue to accept the inferior place assigned them by the hierarchy. It appears that women have been so conditioned to accept the status quo that they are reluctant to enter the struggle. If this continues, macho men and patriarchal clergy will prevail.

NOTES

1. A Brazilian sister.
2. Maria Luiza Guedes Costa, interview, March 1995.
3. Cecilia Domezi, interview, March 1995.
4. Frances O'Gorman, interview, March 1995.
5. Ivone Gebara in *The Struggle Is One*, ed. Mev Puleo, (Albany: SUNY Press, 1994), 209.
6. Sonia, interview, February 1995.
7. Maria Cecilia Domezi, interview, February 1995.
8. O'Gorman, interview.
9. Marie Amelia, interview, February 1995.
10. Ibid.

Chapter 11

DECEPTIVE DEMEANORS

Women are like chameleons, they'll kiss you one day and stab you in the back the next.[1]

Who can describe a Brazilian woman? In the last chapter we discovered her to be a victim of the norms imposed on her by her culture and her church and at the same time either a perpetrator or a challenger of those norms. In this chapter we will examine in greater detail what she does to herself and to other women because of this oppressive environment.

"How I see myself is how I treat others," was the insight shared by a sister in the north of Brazil, who told of her long struggle to free herself from a denial of her own femininity and to reach a healthy acceptance of her womanhood. "The more we discover ourselves as women the more we are able to accept other women and let them grow and develop as they are." This woman was not a behavioral psychologist, nor does it take one to understand that women who grow up in a loving, affirming atmosphere are more apt to affirm and validate other women.

It is clear from the information presented in the last chapter that Brazilian women are born into the inhibiting atmosphere of a macho culture and a patriarchal church, neither of which nourishes or respects their femininity. As expected, their struggle against these oppressive forces manifests itself in a variety of behaviors.

Many women in Brazil do not feel they have the capacity to challenge the societal stereotype of women or men. Consequently, when they marry, have children, and become employed, they believe they are satisfied. Most do not expect or look for more.

Following are excerpts from interviews with women living in a *favela* on the periphery of São Paulo.

Question: How do you feel about your place in society?

I feel women are educated to be the keepers of the house and children. Our mothers pass on to us the obligation to be a "good" mother and wife, with all that entails. [Middle-Aged Factory Worker, São Paulo]

I make myself a slave in my own house. Women perpetuate the system because society is machista. It takes a long time. We were raised like that, our mothers were like that. I can create my child differently but he's in this society. If I changed my behavior, I could lose my husband and my house. I'd be discriminated against in my own family. [Young Married Woman, Paraná]

In my house I'm both the man and the woman. I do everything. I have to take the responsibility for both. That's the man I have, what am I supposed to do? Sometimes my husband is in the street and I worry about him. I think that I allow him to do this. I created this situation. I go ahead and do it all so I don't even give him the space to be a man. [Middle-Aged Woman, Bahia]

There was some evidence that these women were becoming aware of their self-imposed oppression. But since there seems to be no one modeling new behaviors, they feel trapped by their own situations and continue to perpetuate the oppressive system.

Question: Why do women feel obligated to do all the household work?

From the time we are little girls we are taught that these jobs are for women. [Young Single Woman, São Paulo]

Sometimes the man may want to help but the woman won't let him because she thinks it's not his job, his obligation. I have a friend whose husband likes to wash the dishes and clean the house, but she won't let him do it because she feels this kind of work is her responsibility.[6]

Question: Do women realize this oppression?

Women educate the children and we create these stereotypes, boys' roles and girls' roles. I ask myself why we continue to do this. [Young Single Woman, São Paola]

If you fulfill your role as a woman that integrates you and satisfies you because you are doing what society expects of you. This is especially true in regard to caring for the children, cooking, and cleaning. Society expects the woman to care for the home. If she works outside the home it's seen as a work to help her husband. When women study, no one sees it as a career, but as something to help her husband. This is particularly true in the popular class. Women in this class don't even think about choosing a profession. [Professional Woman, São Paulo]

My mother had eight children, and she had to find a way to support us and take care of us. I never saw my father do any of this. She worked until 2:00 P.M., worked at night and had a third job. She thought she had to do this because it was her responsibility to support the kids. She thought the children were hers, my father never saw us as his. My father was just the father, nothing else. [Young Woman, São Paulo]

Some women realize their oppression on an intellectual level, but societal, family, and church pressures are so strong they succumb to machistic teachings. A few women have rejected the patriarchal/machistic oppression, but at a great price, sometimes losing their husbands because of their stand. However, these women are neither visible nor numerous enough to present a model for change to the millions who cannot see an alternative to their subjugation.

Question: Why does the mother feel the children are her property?

Women have so little, they feel they have to hold on to their children to feel secure. It's both culture and nature. It's also a burden she has. The umbilical cord is never cut. The woman assumes the role of man and woman if there is no masculine figure. Women who don't have a man in their lives are still oppressed because they have to fulfill all the obligations of both man and woman for their children. This has a lot to do with the poverty in this country and the lack of values. One of the few things left is the responsibility of the mother. [Young Woman, São Paulo]

It's a question of maternity. This is her job, her role. It doesn't matter what her cultural level is, children are her role. So from when a child is born, until it leaves the house a woman has to be restricted to the universe of the house. She has to feed the kids and take care of them. Women can't let go. [Young Woman, São Paulo]

When a woman leaves the house and enters the work world, she doesn't feel she can relinquish certain responsibilities to her husband so she clings to them increasing her own workload instead of sharing them with her husband. Maybe she does this unconsciously, but it is so implanted in her that she really does oppress herself. Many times the man would be more than willing to take the child to the doctor or be home while the wife goes to work, but the woman says, "no, I must be with my child and be a good mother." [Young Factory Worker, São Paulo]

This image of the "good woman" is so ingrained in a woman's psyche that the end result is self-oppression. She conforms to the societal expectation that the only place for women is in the home and to the clerical assumption that the place for women is in the pews. This thinking is reinforced by the patriarchal church, from the pope to the local pastor.

Frequently, women display the demeanor of the "good woman" because they do not want to lose favor with either their husbands or their priest. They avoid speaking up for women's rights, challenging macho and patriarchal behavior, or creating unpleasant confrontations that might break off relationships with men. Because of this mentality, women oppress themselves and other women as well. This behavior extends beyond the home to the church and the base communities.

A Methodist minister talked about how her female colleagues sided with the bishop against her when she was reprimanded for carrying out her ministry in a feminine way, different from the approved male norm. She thought these women did not want to offend the bishop or lose favor with him. Their jobs were at risk. "When you get hurt by men, it's one kind of hurt," she said, "but when you get hurt by your own gender you feel betrayed."

In the CEBs women experience the same kind of treatment but for different reasons. After Vatican II, women were invited to be trained as ministers, to learn how to speak in public, and to lead the service. Some of the women did not take advantage of these opportunities and showed their disapproval by criticizing women who had the courage to coordinate a celebration, distribute Communion, or give a homily.

A woman in a CEB was barred from participating in the national conference for CEBs. She lived far from the conference site and her husband refused to allow her to travel. What hurt her most, she said, was that the women in the CEB, which was supposed to be a new way of being church, would not support her right to participate against the wishes of her husband. Her challenge of the machistic culture threatened these "good women." By preventing her from attending the encounter, they oppressed themselves as well.

There is no distinction between the face of the "good woman" and the face of the "self-oppressor." To be a "good woman" is to obey, keep silent, and not question male decisions, which results in self-oppression.

One sister commented on difficulties she experienced in trying to raise the consciousness of women today to the ways they are oppressed and how they oppress themselves. "The problem is many women, out of fear, do not permit themselves opportunities to grow or have pleasure. When they have time they sit in front of the television and escape into a world unlike their own."

One group of women, while reflecting on the different ways they felt they were oppressed by men, began to share their experiences of also being oppressed by women as well as how they oppressed other women:

> At one time I thought it was women who were oppressed by men, until I discovered I was looking at the wrong enemy. [Professor, Catholic University, São Paulo]

> At times I feel I might oppress women by pressuring them to get into the women's movement. [Sister, Bahia]

> I feel more threatened by women who promote the conservative hierarchical structure. [Married Woman, Salvador]

> We want to feel in solidarity with women, but at the same time, those who are in the avant-garde often oppress those of us who are slower. [Single Woman, Petropolis]

> I think we can be oppressors if we impose our ideas, the way we think, on others. [Older Woman, Telemaco Borba]

> One woman does not accept well the ideas of another woman. [Woman Liturgist, Paraná]

> My feeling is we're always oppressing someone because women always devalue themselves. I think I'm oppressing my daughter right now because I left her with all the work while I'm here. [Woman at Workshop, Petropolis]

This same woman went on to speak again of the cultural bonds that women find so difficult to break:

> Boys always get first place and are seen as breadwinners while girls stay home and cook. Women devalue themselves. There is a woman who cooks for us at the center and still today doesn't even know what her husband earns. He knows everything and says what must be done. She still isn't able to take the first step in valuing herself as an equal person. It's a cultural thing, ideological, ingrained in us. We will only manage to change this after a long process.

Many among the women interviewed spoke of the evils of their macho culture and the clerical patriarchy and how much they desired greater freedom and equality, but few were willing to challenge the status quo. The reason most often given was fear: fear of standing alone, fear of being different, fear of what others would think or say about them, fear of criticism and of insecurity, fear of marginalization in family and society, fear of losing contact with the church. All of this fear flows from women being immersed in a culture of submission as well as being economically dependent on men. Frances O'Gorman offered some insights into the reasons for this fear:

> Women are scared of going against the structure and they try to keep others in. I see two extremes, those who go way out in the feminist way and those who are completely submissive. They jar the nerves of the others. There are all those in the middle who are afraid of moving. They don't have the spiritual freedom to move. They're afraid of losing that contact with the church. They don't go too far because there's no other church. If we go too far we break off with the church and then what? We have nothing.[2]

A group of women from a base community discussed the various aspects of fear in their dealings with one another.

> We're afraid of leaving our own comfortable space. We give our rights to some-body else because we don't want to assume responsibility. We could be partic-ipating together and deciding together, but we don't. We bring something to be discussed but we don't say anything. Sometimes we're afraid of being criticized. Fear is the reason why women who want their space and when there is an opportunity to get it, don't use it. [Older Women in Favela, São Paulo]

> Fear has a lot to do with it. Women don't have as much experience being active and speaking out, assuming responsibility in a wider reality. They assume responsibility in their own house, but when you ask them to do some-thing in the community they refuse. Fear is the problem with women. [Middle-aged Woman in CEB, Petropolis]

> Women are afraid that other women will talk about them if they are different, if they do things against the social customs. [Young Married Woman, Brasilia]

> Acting behind another's back is a lot more common than open conflict. Sometimes if we say something, we're afraid we'll be given more work. We withdraw to protect ourselves, not to solve problems. [Middle-aged Woman in CEB, Paraná]

For the most part, the women who were not afraid to challenge the status quo were sisters or economically independent women. A wealthy woman in the north noted:

One of the major problems is that the church has kept women on the sidelines, curved and bowed down before its structures. It's basically a problem of education and of understanding that these women haven't had the exposure to what it means to be a woman. Or, they receive fragmented ideas so that their consciousness is naive, so they continue with what their mother and grandmother says and they can't think for themselves.

Two sisters who had worked for many years with women in the rural areas reflected on their struggle.

In the diocese we are maginalized because of our strong stand for women and justice. This creates in us an internal resistance to strengthen our convictions even more. We try and find new ways of doing things, a new way of being church. Our constant occupation is not to be swallowed up by this. The struggle is very heavy. Our preoccupation is to motivate other people and bring them into it.

We women have been excluded for thousands and thousands of years. We have to be in solidarity with those calling out who have been excluded. Oppression is very strong among nuns, too. A lot of times we nuns are the most alienated of all women. I speak from my own experience of women in Latin America. The only way to get out of this is through the Word of God.

Although fear is clearly a major contributor to the oppression of women by other women, another problem for women in the church is jealousy. "Everyone is looking for her place in the sun."[3]

Among the things that are destroying the work among women is jealousy. It seems one wants to see the other fall. Women seem to thrive on seeing others make mistakes. They don't even give credit where credit is due. They can't even give a compliment, but criticize each other. They don't motivate or help each other to get better. They never praise work well done. This kills the work and the motivation. It drives competent women out of church ministry.[4]

A catechist gave the example of a woman who had a charisma, the ability to touch people's lives, who could speak out. Others criticized her because she was outshining them. Jealousy is often the source of criticism. "I know I can't do that so I have to make it look like she's no good either."[5]

Among women there is a great tendency to have petty jealousies, be very competitive and envious because one occupies a better place than the other. This militates against friendship and solidarity in society. They hunt for occasions in which they can put another woman down. [Middle-aged Member of Workers' Party, Cidade Dutra]

Women have to learn awareness of their own strengths. They are really very jealous of one another. They need to be confronted and come together and discuss their jealousy. We have to learn to see our own self-worth instead of being jealous of the success of the other. [Young Sister in CEBs, São Paulo]

Women have so little space in this world and church. Isn't this what starts competition? We're fighting to get those few spaces. [Middle-aged Sister, Bahia]

As far as women who oppress other women, there is a lot of jealousy and little thinking. If somebody is doing well, instead of being happy for her we cut her down and cut the responsibilities because she's going to get bigger than I am. Women want to be queens! We have to look in the mirror and take off the mask and see who we are.[6]

Once a woman conquers a certain post she is afraid another woman is going to get it, so women don't want to open up a chance for other women to reach the same position. Sometimes it's women much less capable that get chosen and there you sit available and not looked at. [Young Woman Cataechist, Paraná]

In addition to the role that fear and jealousy play in the oppression of women by other women, there is the issue of power. However, in some cases, fear is justified when power is abused.

When women are ordained in our church the other women are terrible. They are the ones who spy on the newly ordained and tell tales about them. Unfortunately, they have great influence in the community and are doing a lot to keep us from working with the women in the community because they control the money. The women pastors who lean toward feminism and raising the consciousness of women are hardly ever invited to the council meetings where theologies are shared. These conservative women have enough power to keep our names from surfacing as participants. Sometimes they are more macho than the men of our communities.[7]

Even in the small communities, the one who has the key to the Center ends up dictating to everybody else. They get in with the priests and hold the power over other women. [Sister, Telemaco Barba]

Machismo doesn't just work in men, it's in us too. The desire to put yourself forward, to have power, is inside us too. If we don't work on this we're going to repeat the same history, maybe even worse. We're going to be oppressors.[8]

Women have always exercised a very strong power, an underground power. This power is at the same time beautiful in a woman and diabolical. In the name of all external oppression, women have developed this. Women do reproduce in their children this model. I wouldn't call it masculine, but patriarchal.[9]

Clearly, the inhibiting environment of patriarchy and machismo is primarily to blame for the depressed condition of Brazilian women. But, from what the interviewees have shared, it is also clear that other factors play a significant part in women's oppression. The fatalistic attitude of many was startling. While complaining about their subjugation, women shrugged off their responsibility to do something about it. Many said, "it's our culture and we can't change it," or "the price is too high." Could the underlying reason for this reluctance to change be a fear of losing touch with the "self" that women know and with whom they have become comfortable? Their attitudes make it difficult for those who have the courage to confront their oppressors, be they clergy, macho men, or other women, to effect even a minimal change.

It appears that Brazilian women are so weighed down by what they fear the consequences of a concerted struggle for equality would be that simply to raise women's consciousness will not be enough. They also need to gain the approval and support of the men. The efforts of women to improve their status are not unlike the efforts of the people in the CEBs to reform the church. The root cause of their problem is not among the women anymore than it is among the poor of the CEBs, but in the structures of society and the church.

The first step in effecting change is for women to raise other women's awareness to what patriarchy and machismo do to women. Secondly, women must raise men's awareness to what patriarchy and machismo do to men and women alike. Tereza Maria Cavalcanti observed, "When men experience what women do there will be hope in society and in the church."[10] But, as long as society and the church operate out of patriarchal/machistic dominance and treat women as inferior, the situation will not change. In such a case, the only hope for women's liberation must come from strong women themselves, role models who dare to confront the evils of both church and society, knowing they will have to pay a heavy price.

NOTES

1. Woman who had worked 30 years in a CEB.
2. Frances O'Gorman, interview, March 1995.
3. Sonia, interview, February 1995.
4. Director of catechists in a small city.
5. Ibid.
6. Maria Cecilia Domezi, interview, February 1995.
7. Heidi Jarschel, interview, March 1995.
8. Domezi, interview.
9. Maria Luiza Guedes Costa, interview, February 1995.
10. Tereza Maria Cavalcanti, interview, February 1995

Chapter 12

REMOVING THE STONES

We can't just stay in our little corner and bow our heads to the Vatican.
We need to be prophetesses and go where there is life![1]

If we reflect for a moment on the story of the women at the tomb in Mark
16:1–11, we gain some insight into how Brazilian women might take
courage and find ways to remove the stones that impede their progress toward
equality in their culture and church. The women of Jesus' time were as severely
impeded by their culture as are Brazilian women today, yet they found ways to
remove obstacles.

> Love and faithfulness were shown in culturally appropriate ways as the
> women waited until the end of the Sabbath before going to anoint Jesus' body.
> At the same time, they moved out of their cultural boundaries because of love.
> Normally, a woman anointed another woman's body while a man did the same
> service for another man. In this case, the women on their own initiative
> undertook this final service of love and respect for Jesus while the men, his
> friends, were in hiding.[2]

By overcoming their fears the women at the tomb were rewarded with the call to
be the first apostles, sent to preach and pronounce the resurrection message.

In previous chapters, Brazilian women described some of the stones that
block their way to freedom and equality both in society and the church: clerical deification, machismo, self-oppression, the male image of God, fear, jealousy, oppressive education/formation, a struggle for power, and a sense of
hopelessness. Though it is difficult for many to see beyond these obstacles,
some women proposed creative ways to begin to remove them. Suggestions
came from the simplest rural women, from educated academics, and from both
sisters and other women.

Following are reflections from sisters in various parts of Brazil on how women can begin to effect change so that future generations will not be blocked by the same obstacles in the church and society:

> Change will come about if women concentrate on raising awareness everywhere they are. I have more than four hundred students and have a great opportunity to effect change. I can pass a consciousness on to my students. Women have these openings in a great number of environments. [Middle-Aged Woman, São Paulo]

> Women need to work toward a new society where roles are diffused and power is decentralized. Everyone can contribute not only in society but in the church as well. In reality women are holding all this together. We will find a new way to be church where everyone will participate, a more democratic way of being. [Older Woman, Salvador]

> In this model of church there isn't room for the gifts of women. We need to talk about a new model because we are just reproducing the old now. We must get to know ourselves as women, how we are different from men, and then put this difference into practice. We need to be different in treating people. This difference will bring about change. There will be a struggle and sometimes the cost will be high. [Widow, Petroplis]

A young sister spoke about her experience at a university and how her own awareness of women's oppression grew during her time there. She noted that it was not in the classroom that she learned the most. It was with a group of women who got together and talked things out. The group put pressure on the men and, because of their demands, the men's attitudes toward them changed. "We can do the same in the church," she said.

Another added that it is a question of education, that women have to start changing their thinking. Also, she said, because sisters do not have husbands to control them, they can be freer to tell a priest they will not accept what he is proposing.

> Our vocation as women is to be prophets. Prophets of the identity of women. We have to be ministers of hope, a hope that has been denied to women in their dreams to be equal. We have to be able to talk about the dignity of women who are excluded and have been excluded for thousands and thousands of years. We have to be in solidarity with those calling out who have been excluded. [Sister, Alagoinhas]

"The problem is," added an older sister, "the unfairness keeps on going. Our dream is to change the structure, not to become priests in this structure." A younger sister elaborated on what those changes could mean. "It is we who believe that this new thing in the church we are looking for is equal space for women," she said. "We should have had it a long time ago. We have to assume our roles, celebrate, and be priests."

There are others who would warn that such an approach is a painful one. A female Methodist minister related:

> The fact that some denominations permit the ordination of women does not mean that these structures have ceased to be deeply *machista*. Therefore, we need to help in the construction of a *new church* that lives out a liberating, hope-filled faith, without discrimination or legitimized oppression.

Possible ways to overcome the obstacles Brazilian women face as they struggle for equal recognition and acceptance in their church and society, along with reasons for hope, also came from theologians, Scripture scholars, philosophers, and educators. They presented a continuum of insights ranging from the high hopes and idealistic assessment of a Scripture scholar who maintained, "In spite of all the oppression of the hierarchy, now is the hour for the feminization of the church; it's happening,"[3] to the pain-filled reality of Ivone Gebara, who, when interviewed, was facing a two-year silencing by the Vatican for her "questionable" theology and writings.

> Now I am alone, we are a very few here and there. We cannot be considered powerful. If 200 women in Brazil were thinking in the same way, I would be much more powerful.[4]

In 1997, after her two-year silencing, Ivone had this to say,

> Re-imagining Human Life, God, evil and salvation in a woman's perspective upsets the authorities of the Roman Catholic Church. Because of that, they invited me to study more theology, to leave for some time my narrow perspective and open my mind to the traditional thoughts of the Mother Church. . . . In the present moment I don't know what those authorities are thinking about me. They are worried about the theology of my friend Father Tissa Ballassurya from Sri Lanka. I hope they forget about me.[5]

Others presented a variety of suggestions and observations. As one psychologist said, "Women must be committed to substituting a more feminine model for the father model. A feminine person in a masculine society scares men."[6]

And a former sister observed:

There is an awakening of women, especially through re-reading the Bible. Women are getting encouragement from it. We have more women studying theology, facing down their sons and husbands who oppress them, breaking down barriers with a lot of patience. I can't say there are many, but there are some. There's a little bit of stagnation among religious, but among laywomen there is great growth.[7]

When asked what her hopes were for the future of this church, Tereza Maria Cavalcanti responded, "If this church continues to survive, she can't survive without women. I hope what happens will be the same as what happened to the gerontological hierarchy in the Soviet Union. It fell apart."[8] With the continuing appointment of strong "Opus Dei" bishops and the priests they train, it would appear that this hope is slim.

Frances O'Gorman said she believes the feminists have opened the door to church renewal but have been rejected because they appear too radical to most. However, she said, a lot of what they have put forward will gradually become a part of the future. "This won't happen," she noted, "unless we question the whole male-oriented structure of the church and society along with the formation of priests and seminarians." What was most disturbing to her were the young Brazilian (macho) priests. "We have to build up the dignity of all people, women as well as men, before we can celebrate together."[9]

The most radical challenges to liberation theology, analysts say, are coming from feminist theologians. Women scholars are demanding an anthropological approach within liberation theology that is not patriarchal, and they are critical of male counterparts who fail to question male domination in the church more forcefully.[10]

According to Gebara, there are two groups of feminist theologians in Latin America. The larger group works in traditional theology and is trying to break it open and proclaim that God has both a male and a female face. They agree with tradition, dogma, the sacrificial structure, and all the traditional feelings about God, but they try to open all this to a feminist perspective. These theologians can work in the universities and publish in Catholic periodicals.

Those in the smaller group are trying to connect with European and North American theologians in saying there are problems in the whole structure of

Christian theology. These theologians say we need to re-image human beings, God, and Jesus. This process does not have great acceptance in the official church.[11]

Elsa Tamez, speaking against male chauvinistic ideology that dehumanizes both men and women, invites her male theological colleagues to join women in this struggle, "so that together we can give birth to a new theology."[12] Gebara expresses the need even more poignantly:

> We need to produce a new theology that doesn't fear discord with tradition. When I read the few texts of Latin American women theologians, I see their fear of saying things that differ from the tradition. Even I have this fear! But in my heart, in my body, in my inner being, I beg to speak differently![13]

Feminist theologians, particularly in Latin America, are encountering the same suspicions, misunderstandings, and distrust on the part of the Vatican that liberation theologians faced in their beginning years. Could it be that the patriarchal church sees feminist challenges as an even greater threat to its power and prestige? Latin American theologian Julio de Santa Ana offers his opinion:

> When men are presented with the possibility of sharing with women in the life of the church, in an equal way, there are really pathological reactions. St. Paul had a problem with women; there is no doubt of this. But the fact that Paul had a problem doesn't give us the right to continue to react to women the way he did.[14]

A group of women, who were from the rural areas but had been living and working in a CEB on the periphery of São Paulo for many years, suggested ways to remove obstacles to women's equality:

> I've worked for seventeen years in the community and now I see there are a lot of these women who haven't caught the idea, and I feel they never will. I think we have to start working with the younger people, those who haven't been involved, to try to analyze the situation because these other people will never change. [Middle-Aged, Married Woman, Bahia]

> We have to somehow influence the women around us and say, this happened to me and I didn't like it, and I did such and such, what do you think of it? We have to get women to start questioning situations instead of just accepting them. [Young Woman, Salvador]

This discrimination against women comes from the pope on down, the bishops, priests and seminarians. They all have the mentality that the woman is there just to serve, wash their clothes, etc. If we ever want to change attitudes we have to somehow change their minds. We have to work on them. We have to be proactive. [Older Grandmother, Telemaco Borba]

We have to transmit to our children a different way of seeing the role of women, what constitutes a good woman, that she is not just to stay in the home, wash clothes and iron. She has a right to study, give her opinion, and become active in public discussions. [Married Woman in Her Thirties, Salvador]

This particular group had come together after a long separation. Their CEB had been dismantled by a new pastor who told them they could not meet in the church anymore because the church was only for praying, not for discussing justice issues. These women highlighted four key ways of changing the future for women:

— start working with younger people;
— get women to start questioning situations instead of passively accepting;
— work at changing the minds of the clergy;
— teach children a new role for women.

As they talked, their own awareness of what they could do was intensified. The women in this CEB had become discouraged and had lost some of their zest for the struggle. They had been deprived of support from the clergy and hierarchy, which made them extremely vulnerable. Our meeting with them infused new life in their struggle, making it difficult to end our discussion. We left them still talking about what they could do to effect change in the future.

The type of experience described by these women is becoming more and more frequent in the Brazilian church. "The church of the base communities is merely a tolerated church," wrote Clodovis Boff. "They're allowed to continue with the permission of the pastor, and he can dissolve them at will, send them all home." Boff said that progress made by the laity, and women in particular, toward stronger participation in church life can be "reversed at a stroke, changed overnight with the arrival of a new bishop or a change of parish priest. Even the most thriving community of participation can be reduced to nought."[15]

If, as some contend, the CEBs as we have known them are diminishing, what do Brazilian women see as the next step? For the most part, they are searching for something new. As one educated woman put it, "The seed is still there and it needs to be watered and cultivated, and from there something new will come." She is encouraged by women theologians, though few in number, who are beginning to stand up and speak out. When such women put forth an argument that is clear, transparent, and without double meaning as a proposal to be studied, it helps advance the cause of women. On the other hand, she indicated that she is discouraged by many sisters in Brazil, who tend to be very obedient and supportive of the priests. "I wish they would be a little more rebellious," she said.

Women from other parts of the country spoke hopefully for the advancement of women. A school teacher from the North said she hopes that as women continue developing in society, they will also begin to move forward in the church and be ordained as deaconesses and priests. She based this hope on women's historical record. "It is women who have taken the message of Jesus and walked in his path, not the men. Men have put us a thousand years in error." Another woman pointed out that because there are so few men in the CEBs women have to be more courageous and take active responsibility in their leadership of the people. That is why, noted Irma Passoni, "It is important to enter into dialogue with the bishops and priests to convince them that the church needs women, that the church would be enriched by their contributions."[16]

It is obvious from all that has been said that Brazilian women face enormous barriers to equality both in their culture and in their church. It is equally apparent that it is women who must remove those obstacles, or at least begin to address them by spreading the "good news" that:

— *machismo* is not ordained by God; therefore, to challenge it and raise their sons differently is not wrong;

— women are also made in God's image, they are not second-class citizens and should have rights equal with men;

— the clergy are not divine, and to challenge and question them is not displeasing to God;

— God is not male but pure Spirit, and therefore the female is equally Godlike; mothers, daughters, and wives are of equal value to God with husbands, sons, and fathers.

Brazilian women's oppression of themselves and of other women stems largely from their deep-seated fear of proclaiming these messages. Hence women's unwillingness even to allow themselves to believe the "good news." If they believe, they will have to act, and the consequences for the few among so many are, as we have witnessed, very painful.

We must remember, though, that discomfort and fear are essential to change. . . . The wonderful counterpart of the pain Gebara must feel as she leaves behind her people to fulfill Rome's dictates, is that the sanctions have made people worldwide—especially women—more acutely aware of the importance of her theology.[17]

From the beginning of the New Testament to the end, women have been told not to be afraid. At the time of the Annunciation the angel said to Mary, "Do not be afraid, Mary. You have found favor with God" (Lk 1:30). When the women went to the tomb to anoint Jesus, the angel spoke to them, "Do not be afraid. I know you are looking for Jesus the crucified . . ." (Mt 28:5). Jesus himself stood before them and said, "Do not be afraid! Go tell the disciples to go to Galilee, where they will see me" (Mt 28:9). The message is not that the women ceased to fear, but rather that their faith and love overcame their fear and moved them to action. In his first epistle, John tells us "There is no fear in love, for perfect love drives out fear. To fear is to expect punishment, and anyone who is afraid is still imperfect in love" (1 Jn 4:18).

As long as Brazilian women continue to expect punishment for transgressing unjust cultural norms or protesting against punitive church regulations, their love will remain imperfect and their fear will dominate and keep them submissive. Perhaps one of the philosophers was correct when she said, "No one discusses love anymore, but we discuss every other topic. To talk about love is to be accused of being old-fashioned. Only love builds, only love unites, only love can change society. We have to operationalize this!"[18]

The challenge is clear to Brazilian women. They must be willing to put aside their fear, jealousy, and desire for power, and love one another in a manner that will support all women when they have to endure insults and shame; nasty comments from men, clergy, and some women; or the abuse or abandonment of husbands. They must be ready to be misunderstood in their struggle to remove the stones that impede their progress toward equality. Rising to this challenge is their only hope for new life in church and society.

NOTES

1. Woman from the north.
2. Ursula King ed., *Feminist Theology from the Third World* (Maryknoll, N.Y.: Orbis Press, 1994), 209.
3. Nilda Nair Reinehr, interview, March 1995.
4. Ivone Gebara, interview, March, 1995.

5. Ivone Gebara, "Brazilian Women's Movements and Feminist Theologies," *WATERwheel* 10, no.3 (1997): 3.

6. Marie Amelia, interview, February 1995.

7. Maria Cecilia Domezi, interview, February 1995.

8. Tereza Maria Cavalcanti, interview, February 1995.

9. Frances O'Gorman, interview, March, 1995.

10. David Molineaux, "Women, Native People Challenge Theology," *National Catholic Reporter,* 15 September 1995, 13.

11. Gebara, interview.

12. Elsa Tamez, "The Power of Silence," in *With Passion and Compassion,* Virginia Fabella, MM, and Mercy Amba Oduyoye, eds. (Maryknoll N.Y.: Orbis Press, 1989), 166.

13. Ivone Gebara in *The Struggle is One,* Mev Puleo, ed. (Albany: SUNY Press, 1994), 213.

14. Julio de Santa Ana in *Against Machismo,* Interviews by Elsa Tamez (Oak Park, Ill.: Meyer Stone Books, 1987), 18.

15. Clodovis Boff quoted in David Molineaux, "Women, Native People Challenge Theology," *National Catholic Reporter,* 15 September 1995, 12.

16. Irma Passoni, interview, March 1995.

17. Editorial, "Ivone Gebara must be doing Something Right," *National Catholic Reporter,* 25 August 1995, 24.

18. Cleide Rita Silverio de Almeida, interview, March 1995.

PART III
THE FACES OF PATRIARCHAL WOMEN

We cannot even begin to imagine how we might construct new bridges between women if women themselves lack critical consciousness of where we stand in relation to the divisions between us.

Caroline Ramazanoglu
Feminism and the Contradictions of Oppression

Chapter 13

MARGINALIZED OR ERASED?

Women have for millennia participated in the process of their own subordination because they have been psychologically shaped so as to internalize the idea of their own inferiority.[1]

The preceding chapters include a description of the major effects of
patriarchal dominance of Catholic women exercised by males and per-
petuated by females in both the United States and Brazil. They also delineate
the efforts oppressed women have made to "shed the shackles" and "remove
the stones" that prevent them from assuming their baptismal inheritance.

This final chapter compares the ways in which women from both countries
respond to their patriarchal conditioning, particularly in their relationships
with other women. The resulting profile of the "female face of patriarchy" illustrates that Catholic women of North and South America look very much alike.

Before reviewing the behavior and testimony of the women who were interviewed and attempting to draw some conclusions, it is important to remember:

> One of the most characteristic and ubiquitous features of the world as experi-
> enced by oppressed people is the double bind—situations in which options
> are reduced to a very few and all of them expose one to penalty, censure or
> deprivation.[2]

As stated earlier, to be considered a "good woman" in the patriarchal church
means women must smile, acquiesce, avoid questioning male authority or pronouncements, be grateful for any minor ministry. In other words, by not occu-
pying any space, by remaining invisible, women participate in their own
erasure. It is clear that both Brazilian and North American women are caught
in this web of deception. The Brazilians are caught doubly because machistic
and patriarchal expectations for women are inextricably intertwined. U.S.

women come from a more independent culture but also are caught in the snare of religious brainwashing from which thirty years of post-Vatican II renewal have not fully liberated them.

On the other hand, women who refuse to be erased and who challenge the patriarchal system to practice what it preaches in regard to justice and equality for women are marginalized by clergy and laity alike. Thus, women are forced to choose either to be erased or to be marginalized. Ivone Gebara in Brazil and Edwina Gately, Carmel McEnroy, and many others in the United States have obviously chosen the latter.

Because the Catholic feminist movement has had a much longer history in the United States than in Brazil, more American women are publicly taking a stand against patriarchal oppression. This is testified to by Gebara:

> Some American women are very courageous and there are others who are very closed. It is more or less like that here in Brazil, but women who are struggling have more support in the States than in Brazil. They are more numerous, can publish in newspapers because of the free society, also the feminist movement is older. Where I am living it is a very small closed world.[3]

Few Brazilian feminist theologians will speak, like Gebara, of patriarchal theology as both violent and sacrificial. She contends, "Unfortunately, the sacrifice is always that of poor people, the marginalized women and children." Her censure by the patriarchal church witnesses to her courageous choice to be marginalized rather than erased.

To live on the margins may be painful, but it also enables Gebara to identify more deeply with the poor and oppressed. "My feminism and my theology try to be connected to the interest of this marginalized population, especially women and children."[4] Paradoxically, this has drawn other women to the struggle. She has received a great deal of support from major superiors and other sisters in Brazil as well as from some women in the United States. "We are small," she said. "We cannot be considered a threat. Rome knows we are weak, but they also know we could be strong, so they try to divide us."

Among Gebara's supporters are sisters who have left their institutions to get closer to the people and to work for women's equality. They have experienced conflict within their congregations and felt excluded because of their position. "In the diocese we are also marginalized," one sister said, "but this creates in us an internal resistance which strengthens our convictions even more."

In North America, many outspoken feminist theologians, Scripture scholars, and other Catholic women refuse to choose silence and oblivion and opt to live on the margins. To be "dis-invited" to speak in a diocese or parish is common for women like Joan Chittister, Rosemary Ruether, Ruth Fitzpatrick, Theresa Kane, and others who address the evils of the patriarchal system and call the church to live the message of Jesus for women. So far, no woman in the United States has been silenced as Gebara has. Could this be because Rome both fears and respects the strength of the Catholic feminist movement in the United States?

Antifeminist women in both countries, while cooperating with their patriarchal conditioning, make excuses for the clergy and either ostracize or attack women who speak against patriarchal injustices. Apparently these women do not regard the institutional church's practices to be in conflict with their faith in the mission of Jesus. They have internalized the stamp of unworthiness imposed by patriarchy and do everything in their power to silence or isolate women who think differently.

A major reason women choose to maintain the status quo in the church, and want other women to do so, is their fear of ridicule, change, and loss of security. The clamor in the United States for a married clergy and women priests threatens "good women's" comfortable place in the church. These women appear to be more interested in retaining their image than in challenging the injustices that face them daily.

Most Brazilian women are paralyzed by their machistic society and face total ostracism if they so much as address the topic of sexism in society or in the church. Frightened women from both countries, who have found their identity within the patriarchal church, become angry at women who promote equality because they fear losing their status, inferior as it is. In different yet similar ways, they indicate they benefit from the oppressive structure and often persecute other women who try to change the system.

Among some women in both countries there seems to be an inherent need to put other women down. Women frequently do not help one another. They criticize each other, thereby working against solidarity. They tend to replicate the patriarchal model by using what little power they have to force other women into submission. By criticizing women who speak for equality and by reporting such "heretics" to the clergy or hierarchy, they marginalize those who have the courage to stand against the tide of clerical oppression.

Women act as tormentors both from the top down and from the bottom up. This was evidenced by an Episcopal woman priest in the United States who admitted she oppressed women because that was the only model she had ever seen in the church. Another example is, the sister in the diocesan office who, behind the scenes, forced the bishop's secretary to resign by overtly oppressing her. Similarly, the women in a Brazilian parish boycotted their Methodist minister simply because of her gender. In another Catholic parish the women jeered and taunted a woman catechist because she gave a good homily and distributed Communion, roles they felt belonged to men only.

The effects of patriarchal conditioning on the formation of women are evident in both countries and affect the relationship between sisters and laywomen even today. Their status as sisters, emanating from a male, militaristic formation, elevated those in the religious orders a step above the laity, and many do not want to "descend" to the level of other women. These sisters continue to contribute to inequality in the church by hanging on to privileges and perks denied to other women. Historically, some teaching sisters have influenced women to believe they are secondary and subordinate, not only to the clergy and other men, but to sisters as well. These efforts to erase women's presence from the church and to marginalize those who do not acquiesce have been both conscious and unconscious.

On the positive side, there are sisters in both countries who have provided a different model by stepping down from their pedestals, refusing to avail themselves of perks and privileges, and earnestly striving to bridge the gap that has separated them from other women for so many centuries.

Most religious communities in the United States have consciously striven to educate their sisters in the spirit of Vatican II and bring them to an understanding of the new concept of their role as "laity" in the church. Differences between sisters and other women have been minimized through consciousness raising; the welcoming of associate members; and the opening of hearts, minds, and doors to the reality of women's equality.

In Brazil, many pre-Vatican II-minded religious communities still exist. Sisters are more likely to be obedient and submissive to the patriarchal church, less likely to question their formation, and still likely to regard themselves as a step above other women. Those communities who have European or North American members are likely to be in the forefront in liberating themselves from the burdens their patriarchal formation has placed upon them.

Certain women in each country can be found who, in their efforts to achieve change, burn with anger against the injustices they are experiencing both in society and in the church and who search for ways to confront these sins. There are also some older women who speak of being tired of the struggle, especially when they find the younger women uninterested and others either silent or indifferent. Also, as society as a whole moves to the right, a third group, strong in number, is emerging in each country with the sole purpose of restoring the pre-Vatican II church.

Leadership among women in Brazil is usually found among the organizers and animators of the CEBs, along with a tiny number of theologians. In the United States, this leadership is found among theologians, Scripture scholars, and leaders of such national movements as Call to Action, Women's Ordination Conference, Future Church, and Women-Church. Because the American movement has had a longer history, there is greater support for Catholic feminism in the United States than in Brazil, where the movement is just beginning.

What can be said about the attitude of women toward their future role in the church? Overall, they seem to be more pessimistic than hopeful. Women in both countries view the attitude and actions of the Vatican as repressive and counter to the vision of Vatican II. As examples, they list:

— the pope's statement against women's ordination;
— the appointment of large numbers of "Opus Dei" bishops and priests;
— in North America, the refusal to approve inclusive language in the liturgy and official language of the church;
— in Brazil, the institutional church's efforts to diffuse the power of the CEBs.

These women also expressed feelings of abandonment by the church. The young feel there is nothing life-giving for them in the church; older women are losing heart because there are so few willing to take up the cause with them. Those who do take a strong stand find themselves marginalized both by the clergy and by other women. Because there are so few ministerial roles for women in the United States, and even fewer for women in Brazil, jealousy often rears its ugly head as women compete for the few spaces available.

Brazilian women in the grassroots movement seemed to express a more fatalistic attitude toward women's advancement and therefore tended to shrug off responsibility to work for change. They are more pessimistic about the reality of church reform in their lifetime. Some of the leaders in the movement said they are worn out in the struggle, do not see the possibility of change on the horizon, and are seeking spiritual nourishment in other places. They do not see ordination for women as the answer in their patriarchal church but are asking one another, "What kind of a church do we want?"

In the United States many younger women see the church as irrelevant and very much removed from or out of touch with the problems they face daily. Most born after Vatican II do not have the idealism of the older women who believe that the institution can be changed, that women and men can work together toward a common good. The inconsistent religious education these women received in the 1960s and 1970s did little to ground their faith in any substantial way. On the other hand, the legalism of the old catechism has been mitigated. The result is that most still do not take courses or pursue advanced degrees in religious subjects. On the other hand, older women-reformers, grounded in the pre-Vatican II church, are supplementing their education with advanced degrees in theology, which helps them advance the cause of women. Younger women, however, believe it is foolish to expect the church to embody their hopes and ideals.

Women in Brazil who try to organize for reform are often paralyzed by fear of punishment. This is not so apparent in the United States, where fear is associated more with being ridiculed or losing status and favor.

On the positive side, women in both countries are finding ways to remove the obstacles put before them by clergy and other women. To name just a few, women are now:

— raising one another's awareness;
— experimenting with new models of church;
— availing themselves of feminist education;
— questioning unjust situations;
— teaching their daughters that women are equal;
— giving one another voice through support and encouragement;
— mentoring, collaborating, and empowering one another;
— assuming ministerial roles wherever and whenever possible.

After centuries of bondage, many women today are experiencing a desire for liberation, a hope that they will be set free.

> There are so many who are searching, faltering, knocking themselves against stumbling blocks, and who desperately want to know how they, too, will be able to talk. No, we're not talking about marching, nor processing, nor marking time—what we want is (to walk) with un-bound feet.[6]

Theologians and other feminist leaders in both countries are well aware that the status quo is comfortable, safe, and easy, and that the cost of breaking out of the mold of being a "good woman" can be terribly high. However, they are encouraging women to search for what unites them, to acknowledge one another as full human beings, to speak out for justice, and to choose to be marginalized rather than erased.

Women in both countries must take heed of Gerda Lerner's warning that patriarchy functions only with the cooperation of women, through their continued acceptance and embrace of a system we now know to be oppressive to all, women and men alike. Women must stop thinking of themselves only as "victims" and start examining their role as "perpetrators" of patriarchy.

The number of women studying theology or working as ministers in the church is growing daily and is a major source of hope. "Therefore, all you women, you can take comfort: the church needs you! You are the blood transfusion [this] worn-out body needs, though maybe the body itself does not realize it yet."[7] Like the Canaanite woman in the gospel, today's Catholic women will not go away. They ground their hope in God's promises. The assurance God gave to Moses that the people of Israel would be freed from the Egyptians can be paraphrased for women today. In Exodus 3:7–8 women could read:

> The Lord said, I have witnessed the affliction of women in the church and have heard their cry of complaint against their oppressors, so I know well what they are suffering. Therefore I have come down to rescue them from the hands of patriarchy and lead them out of that land into a good and spacious land flowing with milk and honey, the land of codiscipleship.[8]

NOTES

1. Caroline Ramazanoglu, *Feminism and the Contradictions of Oppression* (London: Routledge, 1989), 137.
2. Gerda Lerner, *The Creation of Patriarchy* (New York: Oxford University Press, 1986), 218.
3. Marilyn Frye, *The Politics of Reality: Essays in Feminist Theory* (Freedom, Calif.: Crossing Press, 1983), 11.
4. Ivore Gebara, interview, March 1995.
5. Ivore Gebara, "Brazilian Women's Movements and Feminist Theologies," *WATERwheel* 10, no. 3 (1997): 3.
6. Barbel von Wartenberg-Potter, *We Will not Hang Our Harps on the Willows* (Geneva, Switzerland: World Council of Churches Publications, 1987), 51.
7. Ibid., 39.
8. Adapted from *The New American Bible, St. Joseph Edition* (New York: Catholic Book Publishing Company, 1970), 61.

Epilogue

The Female Face in Patriarchy

What have you learned about your own participation in the promotion of patriarchy?

What role do you think women play in fostering their own and others' oppression in the church?

What are some practical things you can do to eradicate the female face of patriarchy?

Can you identify ways that you oppress other women?

Why do you think so many women cannot agree to disagree agreeably?

BIBLIOGRAPHY

Abbott, Walter M., ed. "Pastoral Constitution on the Church in the Modern World." *The Documents of Vatican II.* New York: America Press, 1966.

Altman, Lori. "Exodus: The Symbolic Strength of Women," Translated from *Tempo e Presenca*, March/April 1991.

Aquino, Maria Pilar. *Our Cry for Life.* Maryknoll, N.Y.: Orbis Press, 1993.

Augustine. *De Trinitate.* 12.7.10 PL 42.1003. As cited in Maryanne Cline Horowitz, "The Image of God in Man—Is Woman Included?" *Harvard Theological Review* 72, no. 304 (July–Oct 1979).

Azevedo, Marcello de C., SJ. *Basic Ecclesial Communities in Brazil.* Washington, D.C.: Georgetown University Press, 1987.

Banner, Lois W. *Elizabeth Cady Stanton: A Radical for Women's Rights,* Oscar Handlin, ed. Boston: Little Brown and Co., 1980.

Beschin, Giuseppe, trans. *La Trinita.* Rome: Citta Nuova Editrice, 1973.

Bingemer, Maria Clara. "De la teologia del laicado a la teologia del bautismo." *Paginas* 86 (1987).

————."Women in the Future of the Theology of Liberation." *SEDOS Bulletin* 22 (February 1990).

————. "Women and the Theology of Liberation." *LADOC* 23 (Lima, Peru: New Keyhole Series, Nov/Dec 1992).

Boff, Leonardo. *Ecclesiogenesis: The Base Communities Reinvent the Church.* Maryknoll, N.Y.: Orbis Press, 1986.

————. "Quem tem Medo da Igreja Poplar?" in *Revista de Cultra Vozes,* no. 4 (May 1993).

Brown, Joanne Carlson, and Carole R. Bohn, eds. *Christianity, Patriarchy and Abuse.* New York: Pilgrim Press, 1989.

Buck, Claire, ed. *The Bloomsbury Guide to Women's Literature.* New York: Bloomsbury Publishing, 1992.

Busby, Margaret, ed. *Daughters of Africa.* New York: Ballantine Books, 1992.

Carr, Anne E., BVM. *Transforming Grace.* San Francisco: Harper & Row, 1988.

Chittister, Joan, OSB. "Police Protect Church from Onslaught of Women Praying for Church Justice." *National Catholic Reporter.* 23 December 1994.

———. *Winds of Change: Women Challenge Church.* Kansas City: Sheed & Ward, 1986.

———. *Woman Strength: Modern Church, Modern Woman.* Kansas City: Sheed & Ward, 1990.

Chopp, Rebecca S. *The Power to Speak: Feminism, Language God.* New York: Crossroad, 1989.

Christ, Carol P., and Judith Plaskow, eds. *Womanspirit Rising: A Feminist Reader in Religion.* San Francisco: Harper & Row, 1979.

Coll, Regina A., CSJ. *Christianity and Feminism in Conversation.* Mystic, Conn.: Twenty-Third Publications, 1994.

Collins, Mary, RSM. "Women in Relation to the Institutional Church." Address given to the National Assembly of the Leadership Conference of Women Religious, Albuquerque, N.M., August, 1991.

Costa, Ruy O., ed. *One Faith, Many Cultures.* Maryknoll, N.Y.: Orbis Press, 1988.

Crosby, Michael, OFM. *Spirituality of the Beatitudes.* Maryknoll, N.Y.: Orbis Press, 1981.

Daly, Mary. *Beyond God the Father: Toward a Philosophy of Women's Liberation.* Boston: Beacon Press, 1973.

———. *Gyn/Ecology—The Metoethics of Radical Feminism.* Boston: Beacon Press, 1978.

de Lima, Silva. In *The Struggle is One,* Mev Puelo, ed. Albany, N.Y.: SUNY Press, 1994.

de Rosario Lino, Maria. "The Feminine Aspect of God Present in the Fraternity Campaign." *LADOC.* 20 (Lima, Peru: New Keyhole Series, Nov/Dec, 1989).

de Santa Ana, Julio. In *Against Machismo.* Interviews by Elsa Tamez. Oak Park, Ill.: Meyer Stone Books, 1987.

D'Lorenzo, Emmanuel, O.M.I., *Sacrament of Orders* in "Does the Church Discriminate Against Women on the Basis of their Sex?" by Catherine Beaton. *Critic* (June-July 1966).

Dunfee, Susan Nelson. *Beyond Servanthood: Christianity and the Liberation of Women*. Lanham, Md.: University Press of America, 1989.

Fabella, Virginia, M. M., and Mercy Amba Oduyoye, eds. *With Passion and Compassion: Third World Women Doing Theology*. Maryknoll, N.Y.: Orbis Press, 1989.

Fanusie, Lloyda. "Women and the Church (Protestant)." Paper presented at EATWOT Women's Commission. Port Harcourt, Nigeria, August 1986.

Fiorenza, Elisabeth Schüssler. *Discipleship of Equals: A Critical Feminist Ekklesia-logy of Liberation*. New York: Crossroad, 1993.

————. *In Memory of Her: A Feminist Theological Reconstruction of Christian Origins*. New York: Crossroad, 1983.

————. *Jesus: Miriam's Child, Sophia's Prophet*. New York: Continuum, 1994.

Fox, Thomas C. "Fitzpatrick Resigns as WOC Coordinator." *National Catholic Reporter* 32, no. 10 (29 December 1995/5 January 1996): 5.

————. *Sexuality and Catholicism*. New York: George Braziller, 1995.

Freire, Paulo. *Pedagogy of the Oppressed*. New York: Seabury Press, 1974.

————. *Pedagogy of the Oppressed*. New York: Continuum Publishing Co., 1993.

Frye, Marilyn. *The Politics of Reality: Essays in Feminist Theory*. Freedom, Calif.: Crossing Press, 1983.

Gebara, Ivone. "Brazilian Women's Movements and Feminist Theologies." *WATERwheel* 10, no.3 (1997).

————. "Local Church: Practices and Theologies, Reflections From Brazil." *SEDOS* 22, no. 4 (15 April 1990).

————. In *The Struggle is One*, Mev Puelo, ed. Albany, N.Y.: SUNY Press, 1994.

————. "Women Doing Theology in Latin America." In *Feminist Theology From the Third World*, Ursula King, ed. Maryknoll, N.Y.: Orbis Press, 1994.

————, and Maria C. Bingemer. *Mary: Mother of God, Mother of the Poor*. Maryknoll, N.Y.: Orbis Press, 1989.

Gray, Elizabeth Dodson. *Patriarchy as a Conceptual Trap*. Wellesley, Mass.: Roundtable Press, 1982.

Greeley, Andrew M. *The Catholic Myth: The Behavior and Myths of American Catholics*. New York: Charles Scribner's Sons, 1990.

Henry, Sherrye. *The Deep Divide: Why American Women Resist Equality.* New York: Macmillan, 1994.

Hume, Maggie. "Defending Lives, Brazilian Theologian Ivone Gebara." *Conscience* 5, no. 2 (Summer, 1994).

Hymowitz, Carol, and Michelle Weissman. *A History of Women in America.* New York: Bantam Books, 1978.

Isasi-Diaz, Ada Maria. "A Mujerista Perspective on the Future of the Women's Movement and the Church." In *Defecting in Place*, Miriam Therese Winter, Adair Lummis, and Allison Stokes, eds. New York: Crossroad, 1994.

Isasi-Diaz, Ada Maria, and Yolanda Tarango. *Hispanic Women: Prophetic Voice in the Church.* San Francisco: Harper and Row, 1988.

Pope John Paul II. "A Letter to Women." In *The Tablet, the International Catholic Weekly*. London: 15 July 1995.

————."On the Dignity and Vocation of Women." *Origins* 18 (6 October 1988).

Johnson, Patricia Altenbernd, and Janet Kalven, eds. *With Both Eyes Open: Seeing Beyond Gender.* New York: Pilgrim Press, 1988.

King, Ursula, ed. *Feminist Theology From the Third World.* Maryknoll, N.Y.: Orbis Press, 1994.

Kolbenschlag, Madonna, ed. *Kiss Sleeping Beauty Good Bye.* San Francisco: Harper and Row, 1979.

————. *Women in the Church I.* Washington, D.C.: Pastoral Press, 1987.

La Cugna, Catherine Mowry. "Catholic Women as Ministers and Theologians." *America* 167, no. 10 (October 1992): 238–48.

Lerner, Gerda. *The Creation of Feminist Consciousness.* New York: Oxford University Press, 1993.

————. *The Creation of Patriarchy.* New York: Oxford University Press, 1986.

————. *The Grimke Sisters from South Carolina; Rebels Against Slavery.* Boston: Houghton Mifflin, 1967.

McBrien, Richard P. "Confusing the Laity." In fellowship of Southern Illinois Laity. Belleville, Ill.: 28 November 1994.

Miller, J.B. "Psychoanalysis, Patriarchy and Power: One Viewpoint on Women's Goals and Needs." *Chrysalis* 2 (1977).

Molineaux, David. "Women, Native People Challenge Theology." *National Catholic Reporter* 31, no. 40 (15 September 1995): 13.

Murphy, Bishop Francis P. "Let's Start Over." *Commonweal* (25 September 1992): 13.

———. "Ivone Must be Doing Something Right." *National Catholic Reporter*, 31, no. 37 (25 August 1995): 24.

O'Connor, Francis Bernard, CSC. *Like Bread Their Voices Rise: Global Women Challenge the Church.* Notre Dame, Ind.: Ave Maria Press, 1993.

O'Gorman, Frances. *Base Communities in Brazil.* Monograph is an extension of a paper prepared for Overseas Ministries Study Center, Ventnor, N.J.; published by FASE-NUCLAR, Rio de Janeiro, December 1983.

———. *Charity and Change.* Melbourne, Australia: World Vision Australia, 1992.

———. *Down to Earth.* Rio de Janeiro: Ecumenical Center for Action and Reflection, 1987.

———. *Hillside Women.* São Paulo: Edicoes Paulinas, 1985.

Ortiz, Bobbye, trans. "Liberation of Women in the Church and Among the People," extracted from "Situacion-Liberacion de la mujer en la Iglesia y en el pueblo," a document published in *Solidaridad.* Bogota,Columbia, November 1983, reprinted in FemPress, Santiago de Chile, February 1984.

Osiek, Carolyn, RSCJ. *Beyond Anger: On Being a Feminist in the Church.* New York: Paulist Press, 1986.

———. "Women in the Church: Where Do We Go From Here?" *New Women, New Church* 16, no. 6 & 17, nos. 1–3, (November 1993-June 1994).

Parvey, Constance F., ed. *The Community of Women and Men in the Church.* The Sheffield Report. Philadelphia, Penn: Fortress Press, 1983.

Pelton, Robert S., CSC. *From Power to Communion.* Notre Dame, Ind.: University of Notre Dame Press, 1994.

Plaskow, Judith. *Standing Again at Sinai.* San Francisco: Harper and Row, 1990.

Puelo, Mev, ed. *The Struggle is One: Voices and Visions of Liberation.* Albany, N.Y.: SUNY Press, 1994.

Ramazanoglu, Caroline. *Feminism and the Contradictions of Oppression.* London: Routledge, 1989.

Rebara, Ranjani. "Challenging Patriarchy." In *Feminist Theology From the Third World,* Ursula King, ed. Maryknoll, N.Y.: Orbis Press, 1994.

Ress, Mary Judith. "Feminist Theologians Challenge Churches on Patriarchal Structures." First appearing in a special issue of Latinamerica Press, March 1984.

Richard, Pablo. "La iglesia que nace en America Central," *Christianismo y Sociedad* 79 (1984).

Riley, Maria. *Transforming Feminism*. Kansas City, Mo.: Sheed and Ward, 1989.

Rohr, Richard. *Simplicity: The Art of Living*. New York: Crossroad, 1991.

Rowland, Robyn, ed. *Women Who Do and Women Who Don't Join the Women's Movement*. Boston: Routledge & Kegan Paul, 1984.

Ruether, Rosemary Radford. "Can Women Stay in the Church?" *CHURCHWATCH* (August-September 1994).

————. *Sexism and God-Talk: Toward a Feminist Theology*. Boston: Beacon Press, 1988.

————. "Sexism as Idealogy and Social System: Can Christianity Be Liberated from Patriarchy?" In *With Both Eyes Open: Seeing Beyond Gender,* Patricia Altenbernd Johnson and Janet Kalven, eds. New York: Pilgrim Press, 1988.

————. *Women-Church: Theory and Practice*. San Francisco: Harper and Row, 1985.

Russell, Letty M., Katie Geneva Cannon, Ada Maria Isasi-Diaz, Kwok Pui-Lan, eds. *Inheriting Our Mothers' Gardens: Feminist Theology in Third World Perspective*. Philadelphia: Westminster Press, 1988.

Schaef, Anne Wilson. *Women's Reality: An Emerging Female System in a White Male Society*. Minneapolis: Winston Press, 1981.

Schneiders, Sandra M., IHM. *Beyond Patching: Faith and Feminism in the Catholic Church*. New York: Paulist Press, 1991.

Sherrill, Jeanette R. *Power and Authority: Issues For Women Clergy as Leaders*. New York: Hartford Seminary, 1991.

Smith, Amanda. "Most Women Want to Share Power, not Dominate Men." *South Bend Tribune,* 5 December 1993, F2.

Smith, Hedrick. *The Power Game: How Washington Works*. New York: Random House, 1988.

Stanton, Elizabeth Cady. *The Woman's Bible*. New York: European Publishing Company, 1895–98.

Starr, Tama, comp. *The Natural Inferiority of Women: Outrageous Pronouncements by Misguided Males*. New York: Poseidon Press, 1991.

Stuhlmueller, Carol, ed. *Women and Priesthood*. Collegeville, Minn.: Liturgical Press, 1978.

Tamez, Elsa. *Against Machismo*. Oak Park, Ill.: Meyer-Stone Books, 1987.

————. "The Power of Silence." In *With Passion and Compassion,* Virginia Fabella, M. M. and Mercy Amba Oduyoye, eds. Maryknoll, N.Y.: Orbis Press, 1989.

————. *Through Her Eyes: Women's Theology in Latin America.* Maryknoll, N.Y.: Orbis Press, 1988.

Torres, Sergio, and John Eagleson, eds. *The Challenge of Basic Christian Communities.* Maryknoll, N.Y.: Orbis Press, 1988.

von Wartenberg-Potter, Barbel. *We Will Not Hang Our Harps on the Willows.* Geneva, Switzerland: World Council of Churches Publications, 1987.

Wartenberg, Thomas E. *The Forms of Power: From Domination to Transformation.* Philadelphia: Temple University Press, 1990.

Weaver, Mary Jo. *New Catholic Women: A Contemporary Challenge to Traditional Religious Authority.* San Francisco: Harper & Row, 1985.

Welch, Sharon D. *Communities of Resistance and Solidarity.* Maryknoll, N.Y.: Orbis Press, 1985.

————. *Women for What World? In What Church?* 15th General Assembly of the Canadian Religious Conference, Ottawa, 1985.

Winter, Miriam Therese, Adair Lummis, and Allison Stokes, eds. *Defecting in Place.* New York: Crossroad, 1994.

Woolf, Virginia. *A Room of One's Own.* New York: Harcourt, Brace and Company, 1929.

INDEX